ASSESSMENT

HARCOURT SCIENCE

GUIDE

Harcourt School Publishers

Orlando • Boston • Dallas • Chicago • San Diego

www.harcourtschool.com

Printed in the United States of America

ISBN 0-15-313184-5

3 4 5 6 7 8 9 10 082 2002 2001 2000

Harcourt

Contents

UNIT A

Plants and Animals All Around

UNIT B

Living Together

Harcourt

Overview

In *Harcourt Science,* the Assessment Program, like the instruction, is student-centered. By allowing all learners to show what they know and can do, the program provides you with ongoing information about each student's understanding of science. Equally important, the Assessment Program involves the student in self-evaluation, offering you strategies for helping students evaluate their own growth.

The *Harcourt Science* Assessment Program is based on the Assessment Model in the chart below. The model's framework shows the multidimensional aspect of the program, with five kinds of assessment, supported by both teacher-based and student-based assessment tools.

The teacher-based strand, the left column in the model, involves assessments in which the teacher evaluates a student product as evidence of the student's understanding of chapter content and of his or her ability to think critically about it. The teacher-based strand consists of two components: Formal Assessment and Performance Assessment.

The student-based strand, the right column in the model, involves assessments that invite the student to become a partner in the assessment process. These student-based assessments encourage students to reflect on and evaluate their own efforts. The student-based strand also consists of two components: Student Self-Assessment and Portfolio Assessment.

There is a fifth component in the *Harcourt Science* assessment program—Ongoing Assessment, which involves classroom observation and informal evaluation of students' growth in science knowledge and process skills. This essential component is listed in the center of the Assessment Model because it is the "glue" that binds together all the other types of assessment.

HARCOURT SCIENCE

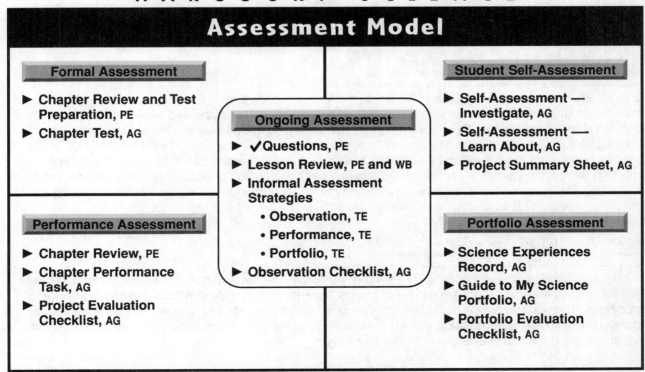

Assessment Model

Formal Assessment
▶ Chapter Review and Test Preparation, PE
▶ Chapter Test, AG

Ongoing Assessment
▶ ✓Questions, PE
▶ Lesson Review, PE and WB
▶ Informal Assessment Strategies
  • Observation, TE
  • Performance, TE
  • Portfolio, TE
▶ Observation Checklist, AG

Student Self-Assessment
▶ Self-Assessment — Investigate, AG
▶ Self-Assessment — Learn About, AG
▶ Project Summary Sheet, AG

Performance Assessment
▶ Chapter Review, PE
▶ Chapter Performance Task, AG
▶ Project Evaluation Checklist, AG

Portfolio Assessment
▶ Science Experiences Record, AG
▶ Guide to My Science Portfolio, AG
▶ Portfolio Evaluation Checklist, AG

(**Key:** PE=Pupil Edition; TE=Teacher's Edition; AG=Assessment Guide; WB=Workbook)

Harcourt

Grade 1

Assessment Components

Formal Assessment

Research into the learning process has shown the positive effects of periodic review. To help you reinforce and assess mastery of chapter objectives, *Harcourt Science* includes both reviews and tests. You will find the Chapter Review and Test Preparation in the pupil book and the Chapter Test in this **Assessment Guide.** Answers to both assessments, including sample responses to open-ended items, are provided.

Performance Assessment

Science literacy involves not only what students know but also how they think and how they do things. Performance tasks provide evidence of students' ability to use science process skills and critical thinking skills to complete an authentic problem-solving task. A performance task is included in each chapter review. Another follows the Chapter Test in this **Assessment Guide.** Each includes teacher directions and a scoring rubric. Also in this booklet, you will find the Project Evaluation Checklist (p. AGxviii), for evaluating unit projects.

Ongoing Assessment

Opportunities abound for observing and evaluating student growth during regular classroom instruction in science. *Harcourt Science* supports this informal, ongoing assessment in several ways: Within each lesson in the **Pupil Edition** (grades 3–6), there are boldface ✔ questions at the end of sections to help you assess students' immediate recall of information. Then, at the end of each lesson, there is a Lesson Review to help you evaluate how well students grasped the concepts taught. The Lesson Review also includes a multiple-choice "test prep" question. In grades 1 and 2, caption questions and Think About It after every lesson are tools for ongoing assessment. Additional material for reviewing the lesson is provided in the **Workbook.**

The **Teacher's Edition** offers Informal Assessment Strategies. These strategies, which appear at point of use within chapters, give ideas for integrating classroom observation, performance assessment, and portfolio assessment with instruction. Located in this **Assessment Guide** is yet another tool, the Observation Checklist (pp. AGxiv), on which you can record noteworthy classroom observations.

Student Self-Assessment

Self-assessment can have significant and positive effects on student achievement. To achieve these effects, students must be challenged to reflect on their work and to monitor, analyze, and control their own learning. Located in this **Assessment Guide** are two checklists designed to do just that. One is Self-Assessment— Investigate (p. AGxvi), which leads students to assess their performance and growth in science skills after completing Investigate in the **Pupil Edition.** The second is Self-Assessment— Learn About (p. AGxvii), a checklist to help the student reflect on instruction in a particular lesson or chapter in *Harcourt Science*. Also in this booklet, following the checklists, you will find the Project Summary Sheet (p. AGxix), on which students describe and evaluate their own science projects.

Portfolio Assessment

In *Harcourt Science*, students may create their own portfolios. The portfolio holds self-selected work samples that the student feels represent gains in his or her understanding of science concepts and use of science processes. The portfolio may also contain a few required or teacher-selected papers. Support materials are included in this **Assessment Guide** (pp. AGxx–AGxxiv) to assist you and your students in developing portfolios and in using them to evaluate growth in science skills.

Harcourt

Formal Assessment

Formal assessment is an essential part of any comprehensive assessment program because it provides an objective measure of student achievement. This traditional form of assessment typically consists of reviews and tests that assess how well students understand, communicate, and apply what they have learned. This is the type of assessment that is typically used in state and local standardized tests in science.

Formal Assessment in *Harcourt Science*

Formal assessment in the *Harcourt Science* program includes the following measures: Chapter Review in **Pupil Edition** grades 1 and 2; Chapter Review and Test Preparation in **Pupil Edition** grades 3–6; and Chapter Assessments in this **Assessment Guide.** The purpose of the review is to assess and reinforce not only chapter concepts and science skills but also students' test-taking skills. The purpose of the Chapter Assessments is, as with other formal assessments, to provide an objective measure of student performance. Answers to chapter reviews, including sample responses to open-ended items, are located in the Teacher's Edition, while answers to chapter tests are located in the Answer Key in this booklet.

Types of Review and Test Items

Students can be overwhelmed by the amount of information on a test and uneasy about how to answer different types of test questions about this information. The Chapter Review and Test Preparation is designed to help familiarize students with the various item formats they may encounter: *multiple-choice items* (with a question stem; sentence fragment; graph, table, map, model, or picture; or using negatives such as *not, least,* and so on), *open-ended items* (which require the student to write a short answer, to record data, or to order items), and *scenarios,* in which the student is asked to respond to several items in either a multiple-choice or open-ended format.

Test-Taking Tips

Harcourt Science offers test-taking tips—aimed at improving student performance on formal assessment—in the Teacher's Edition. The section titled Test Prep—Test-Taking Tips spells out what students can do to analyze and interpret multiple-choice or open-ended types of questions. Each tip suggests a strategy that students can use to help them come up with the correct answer to an item. Included in the section are tips to help students

- ▶ focus on the question.
- ▶ understand unfamiliar words.
- ▶ identify key information.
- ▶ analyze and interpret graphs, charts, and tables.
- ▶ eliminate incorrect answer choices.
- ▶ find the correct answer.
- ▶ mark the correct answer.

The tips include the following suggestions:

- ▶ Scan the entire test first before answering any questions.
- ▶ Read the directions slowly and carefully before you begin a section.
- ▶ Begin with the easiest questions or most familiar material.
- ▶ Read the question and *all* answer options before selecting an answer.
- ▶ Watch out for key words such as *not, least,* and so on.
- ▶ Double-check answers to catch and correct errors.
- ▶ Erase all mistakes completely and write corrections neatly.

Test Preparation

Students perform better on formal assessments when they are well prepared for the testing situation. Here are some things you can do before a test to help your students do their best work.

- ▶ Explain the nature of the test to students.
- ▶ Suggest that they review the questions at the end of the chapter.
- ▶ Remind students to get a good night's sleep before the test.
- ▶ Discuss why they should eat a balanced meal beforehand.
- ▶ Encourage students to relax while they take the test.

Harcourt

Grade 1

Performance Assessment

Teachers today have come to realize that the multiple-choice format of traditional tests, while useful and efficient, cannot provide a complete picture of students' growth in science. Standardized tests may show what students know, but they are not designed to show how they *think and do things*—an essential aspect of science literacy. Performance assessment, along with other types of assessments, can supply the missing information and help balance your assessment program.

An important feature of performance assessment is that it involves a hands-on activity to solve a situational problem. An advantage of this type of assessment is that students often find it more enjoyable than the traditional paper-and-pencil test. Another advantage is that it models good instruction: students are assessed as they learn and learn as they are assessed.

Performance Assessment in *Harcourt Science*

The performance task, science project, and other hands-on science activities provide good opportunities for performance assessment. The performance task is particularly useful because it provides insights into the student's ability to apply key science process skills and concepts taught in the chapter.

At grades 3–6, *Harcourt Science* provides performance assessment in the Chapter Review and Test Preparation feature in the pupil book and in the Chapter Test in this **Assessment Guide**. In the review at grades 1 and 2, the performance assessment is the last item of the Chapter Review; in the test, it is a performance task. The Project Evaluation Checklist (p. AGxviii) is a measure you can use to evaluate unit projects.

Administering Performance Tasks

Unlike traditional assessment tools, performance assessment does not provide standardized directions for its administration or impose specific time limits on students, although a time frame is suggested as a guideline. The suggestions that follow may help you define your role in this assessment.

▶ *Be prepared.*

A few days before students begin the task, read the Teacher's Directions and gather the materials needed.

▶ *Be clear.*

Explain the directions for the task; rephrase them as needed. Also, explain how students' performance will be evaluated. Present the rubric you plan to use and explain the performance indicators in language your students understand.

Harcourt

► **Be encouraging.**

Your role in administering the assessments should be that of a coach—motivating, guiding, and encouraging students to produce their best work.

► **Be supportive.**

You may assist students who need help. The amount of assistance needed will depend on the needs and abilities of individual students.

► **Be flexible.**

All students need not proceed through the performance task at the same rate and in the same manner. Allow them adequate time to do their best work.

► **Involve students in evaluation.**

Invite students to join you as partners in the evaluation process, particularly in development or modification of the rubric.

Rubrics for Assessing Performance

A well-written rubric can help you score students' work accurately and fairly. Moreover, it gives students a better idea of what qualities their work should exhibit *before* they begin a task.

Each performance task in the program has its own rubric. The rubric lists performance indicators, which are brief statements of what to look for in assessing the skills and understandings that the task addresses. A sample rubric follows.

Scoring Rubric

Performance Indicators

_____ Assembles kite successfully.

_____ Carries out experiment daily.

_____ Records results accurately.

_____ Makes an accurate chart and uses it to report the strength of wind observed each day.

Performance Indicators

3	2	1	0

Scoring a Performance Task

The scoring system used for program performance tasks is a 4-point scale (3-2-1-0) that is compatible with those used by many state assessment programs. You may wish to modify the rubrics as a 3- or 5-point scale, as your individual needs and circumstances require. To determine a student's score on a performance task, review the indicators checked on the rubric and then select the score that best represents the student's overall performance on the task.

4-Point Scale			
Excellent Achievement	Adequate Achievement	Limited Achievement	Little or No Achievement
3	**2**	**1**	**0**

How to Convert a Rubric Score into a Grade

If, for grading purposes, you want to record a letter or numerical grade rather than a holistic score for the student's performance on a task, you can use the following conversion table:

Holistic Score	Letter Grade	Numerical Grade
3	A	90–100
2	B	80–89
1	C	70–79
0	D–F	69 or below

Developing Your Own Rubric

From time to time, you may want to either develop your own rubric or work together with your students to create one. Research has shown that significantly improved performance can result from student participation in the construction of rubrics.

Developing a rubric for a performance task involves three basic steps: (1) Identify the process skills taught in the chapter that students must perform to complete the task successfully and identify what understanding of content is also required. (2) Determine which skill/understanding is involved in each step. (3) Decide what you will look for to confirm that the student has acquired each skill and understanding you identified.

Harcourt

Classroom Observation

"Kid watching" is a natural part of teaching and an important part of evaluation. The purpose of classroom observation in assessment is to gather and record information that can lead to improved instruction. In this booklet, you will find an Observation Checklist on which you can record noteworthy observations of students' ability to use science process skills.

Using the Observation Checklist

▶ *Identify the skills you will observe.*
Find out which science process skills are introduced and reinforced in the chapter.

▶ *Focus on only a few students at a time.*
You will find this more effective than trying to observe the entire class at once.

▶ *Look for a pattern.*
It is important to observe the student's strengths and weaknesses over a period of time to determine whether a pattern exists.

▶ *Plan how and when to record observations.*
Decide whether to
  • record observations immediately on the checklist as you move about the room or
  • make jottings or mental notes of observations and record them later.

▶ *Don't agonize over the ratings.*
Students who stand out as particularly strong will clearly merit a rating of *3* ("Outstanding"). Others may clearly earn a rating of *1* ("Needs Improvement"). This doesn't mean, however, that a *2* ("Satisfactory") is automatically the appropriate rating for the rest of the class. For example, you may not have had sufficient opportunity to observe a student demonstrate certain skills. The checklist cells for these skills should remain blank under the student's name until you have observed him or her perform the skills.

Harcourt

► *Review your checklist periodically and ask yourself questions such as:*

    What are the student's strongest/weakest attributes?

    In what ways has the student shown growth?

    In what areas does the class as a whole show strength/weakness?

    What kinds of activities would encourage growth?

    Do I need to allot more time to classroom observation?

► *Use the data you collect.*

Refer to your classroom observation checklists when you plan lessons, form groups, assign grades, and confer with students and family members.

Date _____

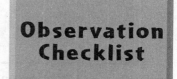

Rating Scale	
3 Outstanding	**1** Needs Improvement
2 Satisfactory	☐ Not Enough Opportunity to Observe

Names of Students

Science Process Skills											
Observe											
Compare											
Classify/Order											
Gather, Record, Display, or Interpret Data											
Use Numbers											
Communicate											
Plan and Conduct Simple Investigations											
Measure											
Predict											
Infer											
Draw Conclusions											
Use Time/Space Relationships											
Hypothesize											
Formulate or Use Models											
Identify and Control Variables											
Experiment											

Harcourt

Using Student Self-Assessment

Researchers have evidence that self-evaluation and the reflection it involves can have positive effects on students' learning. To achieve these effects, students must be challenged to reflect on their work and to monitor, analyze, and control their own learning—beginning in the earliest grades.

Frequent opportunities for students to evaluate their performance builds the skills and confidence they need for effective self-assessment. A trusting relationship between the student and the teacher is also essential. Students must be assured that honest responses can have only a positive effect on the teacher's view of them, and that they will not be used to determine grades.

Student Self-Assessment in *Harcourt Science*

The assessment program offers three self-assessment measures, which are located in this booklet. The first one is Self-Assessment—Investigate: a form that invites students to reflect on how they felt about, and what they learned from, Investigate, a hands-on investigation at the beginning of each lesson. The second measure is Self-Assessment—Learn About: a form that leads students to reflect on and evaluate what they learned from reading and instruction in Learn About at either the lesson or chapter level. The third is the Project Summary Sheet—a form to help students describe and evaluate their unit projects.

Using Self-Assessment Forms

▶ *Explain the directions.*
Discuss the forms and how to complete them.

▶ *Encourage honest responses.*
Be sure to tell students that there are no "right" responses to the items.

▶ *Model the process.*
One way to foster candid responses is to model the process yourself, including at least one response that is not positive. Discuss reasons for your responses.

▶ *Be open to variations in students' responses.*
Negative responses should not be viewed as indicating weaknesses. Rather they confirm that you did a good job of communicating the importance of honesty in self-assessment.

▶ *Discuss responses with students.*
You may wish to clarify students' responses in conferences with them and in family conferences. Invite both students and family members to help you plan activities for school and home that will motivate and support their growth in science.

Harcourt

Name _____

Date _____

How Did I Do?

Investigate was about

_____

- -

_____

How did you do? Circle the word that tells what you think. If you are not sure, circle the **?**.

1. I followed the directions.   **Yes ? No**

2. I worked well with others.   **Yes ? No**

3. I was careful with materials.   **Yes ? No**

4. I completed the investigation.   **Yes ? No**

5. The science skill that I learned was

6. I found out

_____

- -

_____

- -

_____

Harcourt

Name _____

Lesson _____

Think Back!

How did you do? Circle the word that tells what you think. If you are not sure, circle the **?**.

1. I could read the lesson.   **Yes ? No**

2. I used the pictures to help me read. **Yes ? No**

3. I answered the questions
by the pictures.   **Yes ? No**

4. I asked questions when I did
not understand something.   **Yes ? No**

5. I understood most of the ideas. **Yes ? No**

6. I could answer most of the
questions in Think About It.   **Yes ? No**

This is something I learned.

_____
- -
_____

I learned these new words.

_____
- -
_____

Harcourt

Name _____

Date _____

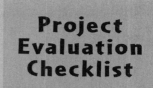
Project Evaluation

Aspects of Science Literacy	Evidence of Growth
1. **Understands science concepts** *(Animals, Plants; Earth's Land, Air, Water, Space; Weather; Matter, Motion, Energy)*	
2. **Uses science process skills** *(observes, compares, classifies, gathers/interprets data, communicates, measures, experiments, infers, predicts, draws conclusions)*	
3. **Thinks critically** *(analyzes, synthesizes, evaluates, applies ideas effectively, solves problems)*	
4. **Displays traits/attitudes of a scientist** *(is curious, questioning, persistent, precise, creative, enthusiastic; uses science materials carefully; is concerned for environment)*	

Summary Evaluation/Teacher Comments: _____

_____

_____

_____

_____

Harcourt

Name _____

Date _____

Project Summary Sheet

You can tell about your science project by completing the following sentences.

My Unit Project

1. My project was about _____
   _____
   _____.

2. I worked on this project with _____
   _____
   _____.

3. I gathered information from these sources: _____
   _____
   _____.

4. The most important thing I learned from doing this project is _____
   _____
   _____.

5. I think I did a (an) _____ job on my project because
   _____
   _____.

6. I'd also like to tell you _____
   _____
   _____
   _____
   _____.

Harcourt

Grade 1

Assessment Guide   AGxix

Portfolio Assessment

A portfolio is a showcase for student work, a place where many types of assignments, projects, reports, and writings can be collected. The work samples in the collection provide "snapshots" of the student's efforts over time, and taken together they reveal the student's growth, attitudes, and understanding better than any other type of assessment. However, portfolios are not ends in themselves. Their value comes from creating them, discussing them, and using them to improve learning.

The purpose of using portfolios in science is threefold:

▶ *To give the student a voice in the assessment process.*

▶ *To foster reflection, self-monitoring, and self-evaluation.*

▶ *To provide a comprehensive picture of a student's progress.*

Portfolio Assessment in *Harcourt Science*

In *Harcourt Science,* students create portfolio collections of their work. The collection may include a few required papers, such as the Chapter Test, Chapter Performance Task, and Project Evaluation.

From time to time, consider including other measures (Science Experiences Record, Project Summary Sheet, and Student Self-Assessment Checklists). The Science Experiences Record, for example, can reveal insights about student interests, ideas, and out-of-school experiences (museum visits, nature walks, outside readings, and so on) that otherwise you might not know about. Materials to help you and your students build portfolios and use them for evaluation are included in the pages that follow.

Harcourt

Using Portfolio Assessment

▶ *Explain the portfolio and its use.*
Describe how people in many fields use portfolios to present samples of their work when they are applying for a job. Tell students that they can create their own portfolio to show what they have learned, what skills they have acquired, and how they think they are doing in science.

▶ *Decide what standard pieces should be included.*
Engage students in identifying a few standard, or "required," work samples that each student should include in his or her portfolio, and discuss reasons for including them. The student's recording sheet for the Chapter Performance Task, for example, might be a standard sample in the portfolios because it shows students' ability to use science process skills and critical thinking skills to solve a problem. Together with your class, decide on the required work samples that everyone's portfolio will include.

▶ *Discuss student-selected work samples.*
Point out that the best work to select is not necessarily the longest or the neatest. Rather, it is work the student believes will best demonstrate his or her growth in science understanding and skills.

▶ *Establish a basic plan.*
Decide about how many work samples will be included in the portfolio and when they should be selected. Ask students to list on Guide to My Science Portfolio (p. AG xxiii) each sample they select and to explain why they selected it.

▶ *Tell students how you will evaluate their portfolios.*
Use a blank Portfolio Evaluation sheet to explain how you will evaluate the contents of a portfolio.

▶ *Use the portfolio.*
Use the portfolio as a handy reference tool in determining students' science grades and in holding conferences with them and family members. You may wish to send the portfolio home for family members to review.

Name _____ Date _____

Science Experiences Record

Date	What I Did	What I Thought or Learned

Harcourt

Name _____ **Date** _____

What Is in My Portfolio	Why I Chose It
1.	
2.	
3.	
4.	
5.	
6.	
7.	

I organized my Science Portfolio this way because _____

_____

_____

_____

_____

Harcourt

Student's Name _____

Date _____

Portfolio Evaluation

Aspects of Science Literacy	Evidence of Growth
1. **Understands science concepts** *(Animals, Plants; Earth's Land, Air, Water, Space; Weather; Matter, Motion, Energy)*	_____ _____ _____
2. **Uses science process skills** *(observes, compares, classifies, gathers/interprets data, communicates, measures, experiments, infers, predicts, draws conclusions)*	_____ _____ _____ _____
3. **Thinks critically** *(analyzes, synthesizes, evaluates, applies ideas effectively, solves problems)*	_____ _____ _____
4. **Displays traits/attitudes of a scientist** *(is curious, questioning, persistent, precise, creative, enthusiastic; uses science materials carefully; is concerned for environment)*	_____ _____ _____

Summary of Portfolio Assessment

For This Review			Since Last Review		
Excellent	Good	Fair	Improving	About the Same	Not as Good

Harcourt

Name _____

Date _____

Living and Nonliving Things

Part I   Vocabulary

Circle the word that answers the question.

1. What do we call hearing, sight, touch, smell, and taste?

ears   hands   senses

Circle the word that names the pictures.

2.

living   nonliving

3.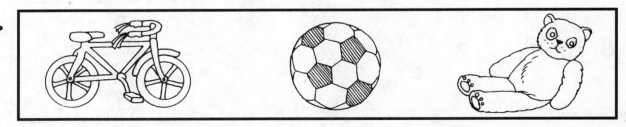

living   nonliving

Harcourt

Name _____

Draw a line from each sense to the child using it.

4. sight •

5. hearing •

6. touch •

7. taste •

8. smell •

Harcourt

9. Circle each word that tells what these living things need.

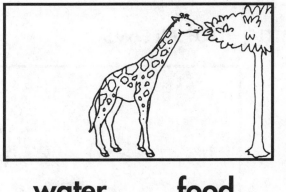

water   food   air   water

10. Circle each word that tells what these living things do.

grows   sees   changes   hears

11. Circle the nonliving thing.

Part III Process Skills Application

Process skills: observe, compare

12. Write **g** under the thing that grows.

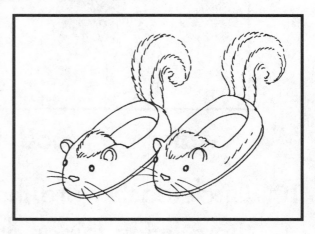

```
_____          _____
- - - - - - -        - - - - - - -
_____          _____
```

13. Write **c** under the thing that changes.

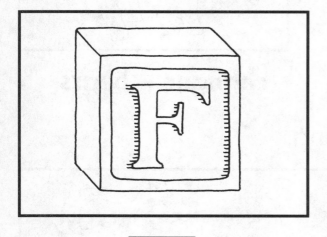

```
_____          _____
- - - - - - -        - - - - - - -
_____          _____
```

Harcourt

Living Things

PERFORMANCE TASK

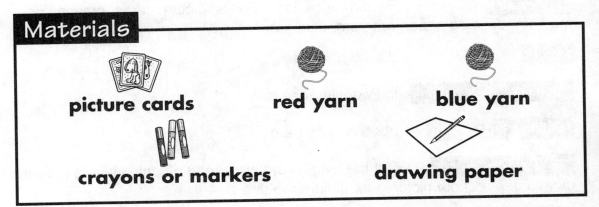

Materials

picture cards   red yarn   blue yarn

crayons or markers   drawing paper

1. Make a red circle and a blue circle with the yarn.

2. Look at the pictures.

3. Put the living things in the red circle.

4. Put the nonliving things in the blue circle.

5. Draw other living and nonliving things.

Living Things   Nonliving Things

Harcourt

PERFORMANCE TASK

Living Things

Materials   Performance Task sheets, picture cards, crayons or markers, drawing paper, red yarn, blue yarn

Time   20–30 minutes

Suggested Grouping   individuals or pairs

Science Processes   observe, compare

Preparation Hints   Cut the lengths of yarn ahead of time. Have a parent or volunteer cut out pictures for children to use.

Introduce the Task   Have children look around the classroom and name the living and nonliving things that they see. Encourage them to say what the living things can do. Distribute materials. Read the five directions to children. Be sure that they understand how to make their circles and what they should put in them.

Promote Discussion   Have children compare their pictures of living and nonliving things. Then encourage children to say what the living things do.

Scoring Rubric

Performance Indicators

_____ Places pictures of things that are living within the red circle.

_____ Places pictures of things that are nonliving within the blue circle.

_____ Draws pictures of living and nonliving things.

_____ Compares pictures with classmates and tells what the living things can do.

Observations and Rubric Score

3	2	1	0

Harcourt

Name _____

Date _____

All About Plants

Part I Vocabulary

Circle the word or words that complete each sentence.

1. Most plants grow from a

   flower   **stem**   **seed**

2. The outside of a seed is its

   stem   **seed coat**   **flower**

Draw a line from the name of each plant part to its picture.

3. leaves •

4. flower •

5. roots •

6. stem •

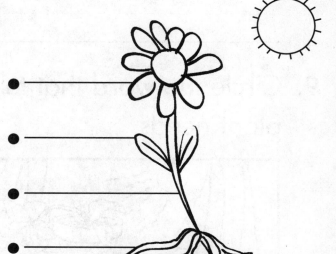

7. Put an **X** on the sunlight.

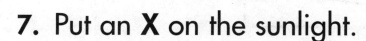

Name _____

We eat parts of some plants.

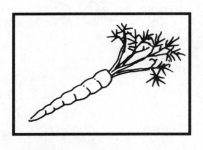      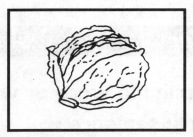

carrot   **apple**   **lettuce**

Write a word or draw a picture to answer the question.

8. Which plant has a root we eat?

   _____

   -

   _____

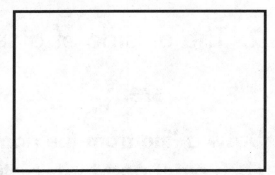

9. Circle the word that tells what this plant needs.

light   water   air

Harcourt

10. Circle what the flowers under
the tree need.

air   **water**   **light**

11. Number the pictures to show
how a plant grows.

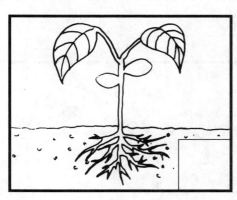
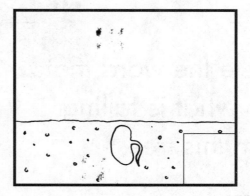

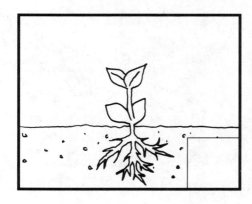
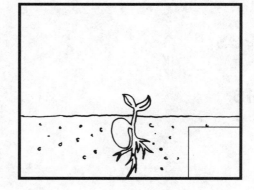

Harcourt

Name _____

Process skills: *observe, compare*

12. Put an **X** under the plant whose
     seed was planted first.

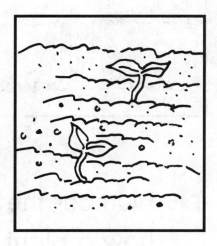

____   ____   ____

13. Circle the word that
     tells what is falling
     from this tree.

stems

leaves

roots

Harcourt

How Plants Grow

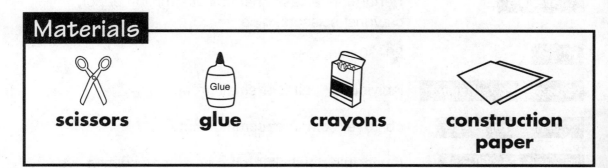

Materials

scissors   glue   crayons   construction paper

1. Draw a picture that shows all the parts of a plant.

2. Then cut and paste the words to name the parts of your picture.

3. Tell your teacher which part of your plant grows first, next, and last.

air	sunlight	water	roots
stem	leaves	flowers	

Harcourt

PERFORMANCE TASK

How Plants Grow

Materials Performance Task sheets, construction paper, crayons, scissors, glue

Time 20–30 minutes

Suggested Grouping individuals, pairs, or small groups

Science Processes observe, compare, communicate

Preparation Hints If possible, take children outside or display a live plant for children to observe. Have children share what they know about the parts of the plant and how it grows.

Introduce the Task Explain to children that their task is to draw any plant they choose and to use the words on the Performance Task sheet to label all the parts of their picture. When they are finished with their drawing, they will use it to explain which part of the plant grows first, next, and so on.

Promote Discussion When children finish, have them compare their work. Ask the class to summarize how different kinds of plants grow.

Scoring Rubric

Performance Indicators

_____ Makes an accurate drawing of a plant, showing roots, leaves, stems, and flowers.

_____ Labels each part of the drawing by pasting the appropriate word next to each part.

_____ Uses proper sequence to clearly explain how a plant grows.

_____ Compares his or her own drawing with those of classmates.

Observations and Rubric Score

3	2	1	0

Harcourt

Name _____

Date _____

All About Animals

Part 1   Vocabulary

Draw a line from each word to the picture that matches it.

1. mammal •

2. amphibian •

3. reptile •

4. gills •

5. tadpole •

6. insect •

7. pupa •

8. hatch •

9. larva •

Harcourt

Part II   Science Concepts and Understanding

10. Circle what all animals need.

   wings   food   fins

11. Circle what helps some animals get air.

   feet   fur   noses

12. Circle the animal that builds its home.

13. Put an **X** on the part of the animal
   that helps it get water.

Harcourt

14. Circle the word that tells what is in the picture.

reptiles

mammals

15. Circle something that only birds have.

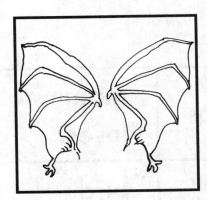 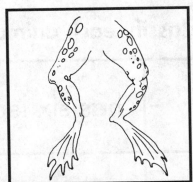 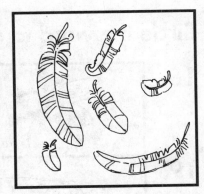

16. Circle something that only mammals have.

feet   **fur**   **wings**

Harcourt

Name _____

Process Skills: sequence, classify

17. Number the pictures to show how a butterfly grows.

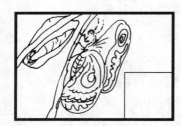
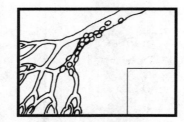

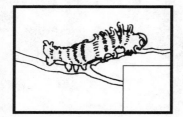

Circle the word to classify each animal.

18.		has six legs	**mammal** **insect**
19.		has wet skin	**bird** **amphibian**
20.		has gills	**reptile** **fish**

Harcourt

Animal Watch

Materials

caterpillar 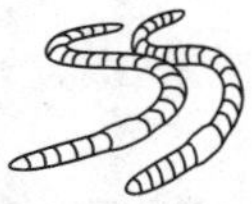   earthworm 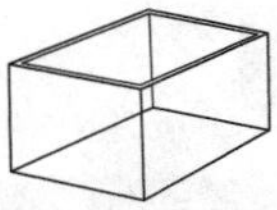   plastic box

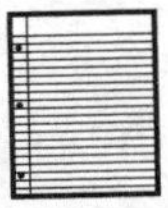

paper

1. Observe the animals in the plastic box.

2. Write their names on your paper.

3. Compare the two animals. Write two ways they are the same and different.

4. Share what you wrote on your paper.

Animals	Same	Different
Caterpillar and Earthworm	1. 2.	1. 2.

PERFORMANCE TASK

Animal Watch

Materials   Performance Task sheets, caterpillar, earthworm, plastic box, paper, pencils, several animal picture cards

Time   20–30 minutes

Suggested Grouping   individuals, pairs, or small groups

Science Processes   observe, compare, communicate

Preparation Hints   Put the earthworm and the caterpillar in the box. Put the picture cards on the chalk ledge. Have the remaining materials ready.

Introduce the Task   Display the animal picture cards one at a time. Encourage children to brainstorm ways to describe each animal. Distribute materials. Read the first direction aloud. Make sure children can identify the animals. Tell children that they will have a chance to describe what is the same and different about the animals. Read directions 2–4 to children. Have volunteers explain what they will do and how they will share the information on their papers.

Promote Discussion   Ask individuals what was the same and different about the animals. Have them count differences class members described.

Scoring Rubric

Performance Indicators

_____ Lists two ways in which the animals are the same.

_____ Lists two ways in which the animals are different.

_____ Writes a clear description of the animals' similarities and differences.

_____ Explains clearly the similarities and differences.

Observations and Rubric Score

3	2	1	0

Harcourt

Chapter Assessment

Plants and Animals Need One Another

Circle the word that answers the question.

1. What is the powder on flowers that helps make seeds?

dust   pollen   hair

2. What is the basket?

clothing   a product

3. What do leaves and worms do for the soil?

dry it   water it   enrich it

4. What do these animals use the tree for?

water   shelter

Harcourt

Part II Science Concepts and Understanding

These animals are meeting their needs with grass.
Circle the word that tells what they need.

5.

water

shelter

6.

air

food

These animals are helping plants. Circle the
words that tell what they are doing.

7.

moving pollen

finding water

8.

enriching soil

spreading seeds

Harcourt

Name _____

Draw a line from each picture to what the
plants or animals give people.

9.  •

                                          • food

10.  •

                                          • shelter

11.  •

                                          • beauty

12.  •

Harcourt

Name _____

Part III   Process Skills Application

Process skills: observe, investigate, classify

Circle the word that tells what each product comes from.

13.

animals

plants

14.

animals

plants

15. Circle the words that tell what the dog is doing for the woman.

hearing for her

seeing for her

16. Write the word that tells what each product comes from.

plant

animal

_____

- - - - - - - - - - - -

_____

Harcourt

How Animals Use Plants

Materials

markers or crayons

index cards

lined paper

This picture shows a
squirrel using a plant
to meet its needs.
Which of its needs is the
animal meeting?

1. List three plants that three animals
   use to meet their needs.

2. Make a picture card to show
   each animal using its plant.

3. Show each card and tell how
   the animal is using the plant.

Harcourt

PERFORMANCE TASK

How Animals Use Plants

Materials Performance Task sheets, markers or crayons, index cards, lined paper

Time 20–30 minutes

Suggested Grouping individuals or small groups

Science Processes communicate, observe

Preparation Hints Count out the cards for each child ahead of time. You may wish to cut construction paper into 4-in. × 6-in. pieces.

Introduce the Task Ask children how a bird uses a tree. Elicit that the tree can be a home; the bird uses it to meet its need for shelter. Ask children to suggest other plants that animals use for food and for water. Distribute the materials. Read aloud the title and the paragraph under it. Have a volunteer answer the question. (It is meeting its need for shelter.) Read the directions with children. Have volunteers tell what they will put on their lists and draw on the cards. Tell children to write their lists on the lined paper. Remind them to share the cards when they finish.

Promote Discussion When children finish, have them show the class another child's card and explain how the animal pictured is using the plant.

Scoring Rubric

Performance Indicators

_____ Lists several plants that animals use.

_____ Draws pictures that accurately depict how the animals use the plants listed.

_____ Explains clearly how the animals use the plants to meet their needs.

_____ Explains what is happening on another child's picture card.

Observations and Rubric Score

3	2	1	0

Harcourt

Chapter Assessment

A Place to Live

Part I Vocabulary

Draw a line to the word or words that complete each sentence.

1. A dry place that gets a lot of sunlight and very little rain is a •

2. A place where the soil is moist and many trees grow is a •

3. A place that is wet all year and has many trees is a •

4. A large body of salt water is an •

5. Ocean plants are •

• **forest**

• **desert**

• **rain forest**

• **ocean**

• **algae**

Harcourt

Part II Science Concepts and Understanding

Circle the answer to each question.

6. What helps these plants grow in the forest?

   moist soil

   dry soil

7. What do these animals find in the forest?

   shelter

   waxy leaves

8. What can these desert plants hold in their leaves and stems?

   soil

   water

Harcourt

Name _____

Circle the words or picture to answer
each question.

9. Where do some desert animals
   get water?

   from oceans   **from plants**

10. Which animal lives in the middle
    level of the rain forest?

11. What covers more than half of
    Earth?

    land   **oceans**

12. What do plants in the middle level
    of the rain forest get?

    cold   **light**

Harcourt

Name _____

Part III   Process Skills Application

Process Skills: classify, compare

13. Write letters to complete this chart.
The top row has been done for you.

d = desert   o = ocean
f = forest   r = rain forest

Animal	Plant	Where They Live
		r

14. Circle the part of the sea turtle
that helps it steer.

shell

flippers

Harcourt

Who Lives Here?

Materials

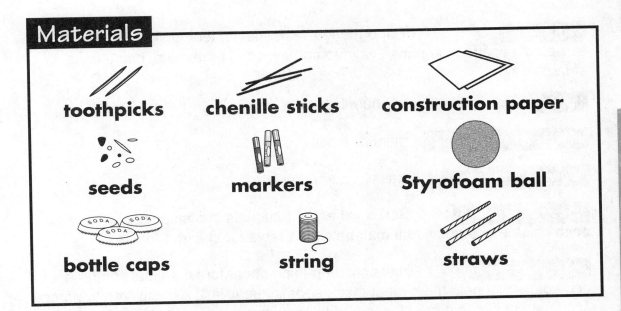

toothpicks   chenille sticks   construction paper

seeds   markers   Styrofoam ball

bottle caps   string   straws

Places to Live

forest   desert

rain forest   ocean

1. Choose one of the places to live.

2. List body parts an animal needs to live there.

3. Make a model of an animal that could live there.

4. Share your model.

Harcourt

PERFORMANCE TASK

Who Lives Here?

Materials   Performance Task sheets, toothpicks, chenille sticks, scraps of construction paper, Styrofoam ball, seeds, markers, bottle caps, string, straws

Time   20–30 minutes

Suggested Grouping   pairs or small groups

Science Processes   classify, communicate

Preparation Hints   Sort a variety of materials into small bags—one for each child. Place additional materials on a table for children to use.

Introduce the Task   Have children think about forest animals and the body parts that help them meet their needs in the forest. Ask children to name animals that live in other places and tell how their body parts help them meet their needs there. Be sure they mention animals of the desert, rain forest, and ocean. Distribute materials. Read aloud the title of the Performance Task and the list of Places to Live. Then help children read the directions.

Promote Discussion   Have children who selected the same place to live compare their animals. Ask the groups to report on how their animals' body parts help them meet their needs.

Scoring Rubric

Performance Indicators

_____ Lists more than one adaptation an animal needs in order to live in the place selected.

_____ Explains clearly what adaptations an animal needs and why.

_____ Makes a model of an animal from scrap material.

_____ Explains to the class how each part of the animal helps it to live in the place selected. For example, their model may show an animal that has strong toenails needed to climb trees.

Observations and Rubric Score

3	2	1	0

Harcourt

Name _____

Date _____

Earth's Land

Part I   Vocabulary

Circle the word that answers each question.

1. What is a hard, nonliving thing?

    rock   **tree**

2. What is made of very tiny pieces of rock?

    soil   **sand**

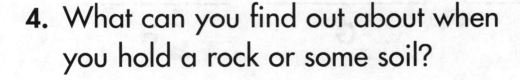

3. What is made of tiny pieces of rock and dead plants and animals?

    sand   **soil**

4. What can you find out about when you hold a rock or some soil?

    its taste   **its texture**

Harcourt

Name _____

Circle the letter next to the word that completes each sentence.

5. One way to sort rocks is by their

      A smell   **B** color   **C** sound

6. Glass products are made from

      F sand   **G** water   **H** air

7. A 🌿 needs soil to

      A move   **B** hear   **C** grow

8. What can people make from rocks?

     F   **G**   **H**

9. Draw an animal that uses soil to
make its home.

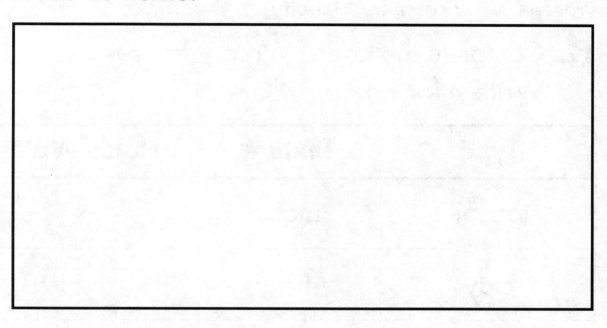

10. Circle what farmers grow in soil.

 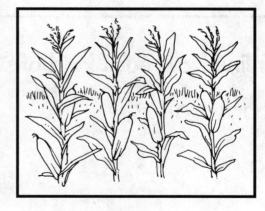

11. Name something that makes
the soil rich.

_____

- -

_____

Harcourt

Name _____

Process skills: compare, classify

12. Complete the chart. Write **y** for yes.
Write **n** for no.

Type	Texture	Holds Water
topsoil	moist	y
clay	sticky	_____
sandy soil	rough	_____

Draw a line from each kind of soil to its color.

13. sandy soil •   • dark brown

14. clay   •   • red or yellow

15. topsoil   •   • light brown

16. What kind of soil is best for crops?

_____

Harcourt

Name _____   Date _____

Soil Test

Materials

6 paper cups   water   topsoil

clay   sand   marker

1. Make a hole in the bottom of three cups.

2. Put topsoil in one cup, clay in another, and sand in the last cup.

3. Write **T** on an empty cup. Hold the cup of topsoil over it. Pour water through the topsoil.

4. Write **C** and **S** on two more empty cups. Pour water through the clay and sand over these cups.

5. Compare the amounts of water in the cups. Put the cups in order from most to least.

PERFORMANCE TASK

Soil Test

Materials	Performance Task sheets, paper cups, marker, topsoil, clay, sand, water
Time	20–30 minutes
Suggested Grouping	pairs or small groups
Science Processes	compare, classify
Preparation Hints	You may wish to have a volunteer measure out the soils ahead of time for each child.

Introduce the Task Help children recall the three types of soil (clay, sand, topsoil). Ask them to say how easily they think water drains through clay, sand, and topsoil. Tell them that they will do an experiment to see how easily water drains through the three types of soil. Distribute materials and have volunteers read the directions aloud, restating what they are to do in their own words.

Promote Discussion When children finish, ask them to report on what they observed. Then call on volunteers to represent clay, sand, and topsoil. Have them arrange themselves in the order of the amounts of water that drain through the three types of soil.

Scoring Rubric

Performance Indicators

_____ Sets up the cups with three types of soil correctly.

_____ Compares the amounts of water that drained through the three types of soil.

_____ Orders the cups from greatest to least amount of water.

_____ Explains clearly that the most water drained through the sand, the next greatest amount through the topsoil, and the least through the clay.

Observations and Rubric Score

3	2	1	0

Harcourt

Earth's Air and Water

Draw a line from the word to the place on the map that it names.

1. lake •

2. river •

3. stream •

4. Color the fresh water blue.

5. Color the salt water green.

6. What do we feel when the wind blows? Circle it.

air   sky   clouds

Part II Science Concepts and Understanding

Circle the letter of the best choice.

7. What lifts a kite into the sky?

A clouds   **B** sunshine   **C** air

8. What do you know when you see bubbles in water?

F The water is very cold.

G You should not drink the water.

H There is air in the water.

9. What must be taken out of ocean water before people can drink it?

A clouds

B salt

C sunlight

Harcourt

10. Circle the picture that does **NOT** show air moving.

Draw a line to the words that best complete the sentence.

11. Most lakes have •   • salt water.

12. The oceans have •   • fresh water.

13. Which kind of water falls as rain?

 _____
- -
_____

Circle the word that best completes the sentence.

14. Before people drink water, they must make sure it is

    cold   **clean**

Harcourt

Name _____

Part III   Process Skills Application

Process skills: infer, communicate

15. Circle the word that tells what is in the bubbles.

    water   **air**

16. How much of Earth is covered by oceans? Circle to show.

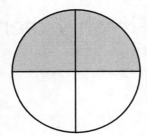 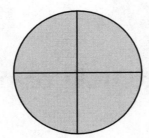 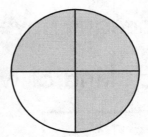

Circle the letter of the best answer.

17. Which thing has no air in it?

    A water   **B** rock   **C** soil

18. Which sense helps you know the air is moving?

    F sight   **G** taste   **H** smell

Harcourt

Animal Kites

Materials

 construction paper   string   paper

 markers or crayons   scissors   tape

tissue-paper streamers

Day	Wind?	What the Kite Did

1. Draw an animal big enough to be a kite. Cut it out.

2. Tape streamers and a string to your animal.

3. Take your kite outside. Hold it by the string.

4. Fly your kite every day for a week. Write down what happens.

5. Make a chart to share what you learn.

Harcourt

PERFORMANCE TASK

Animal Kites

Materials   construction paper, 12-in. pieces of string, markers or crayons, tissue-paper streamers, scissors, tape, Performance Assessment sheets, pencils, paper

Time   20–30 minutes

Suggested Grouping   individuals or small groups

Science Processes   observe, infer, communicate

Preparation Hints   Make enough streamers for each child to have several.

Introduce the Task   Ask children what clues they can look for out the classroom window to find out whether the wind is blowing and how hard it is blowing (for example, papers or leaves blowing across the schoolyard, leaves on trees blowing, people holding onto their hats). Explain that they will be making animal kites that will show whether the wind is blowing and how hard it is blowing. Distribute the Performance Assessment sheets. Help children read the materials list, and have them look at the picture. Ask if they can tell how they will use the materials to make their kites. Help them read the directions. Let children make their kites, take them out to try them, and remind them to record the results. Repeat the procedure each day for a week.

Promote Discussion   At the end of the week, ask children to report what happened each day.

Scoring Rubric

Performance Indicators

_____ Assembles kite successfully.

_____ Carries out experiment daily.

_____ Records results accurately.

_____ Makes an accurate chart and uses it to report to the class about flying the kite.

Observations and Rubric Score

3	2	1	0

Harcourt

Measuring Weather

Part I Vocabulary

Draw a line from each picture to a word or words for it.

1.  •   • water cycle

2.  •   • weather

3.  •   • thermometer

4.  •   • wind

Write the word or words that best complete the sentence.

| water vapor   evaporate   temperature   condense |

5. We call how warm or cold something is its

_____

- -

_____ .

Harcourt

6. Water that you can not see
in the air is

_____

- -

_____.

7. Warm air makes water

_____

- -

_____.

8. Cooler air makes water vapor

_____

- -

_____.

Part II   Science Concepts and Understanding

9. What does a meteorologist study?

_____

- -

_____

Circle the letter of the word that best completes the sentence.

10. At night, with no sunlight, the air is

A cloudy   **B** cooler   **C** warmer

Harcourt

11. Circle the letter of the city **MOST** likely to get rain.

F

G

H

Write the word that best completes each sentence.

| rain   water vapor   condenses   evaporates |

12. On a hot day, water _____.

13. When the drops of water in a cloud get heavy, they fall as _____.

14. Water in the air that you can not see is _____.

15. When water vapor meets cooler air, it _____.

Harcourt

Name _____

Part III   Process Skills Application

Process skills: observe, compare

16. Circle the picture that shows a windy day.

17. Circle the words that tell where the weather is warmer.

Hal's city   **Ann's city**

Harcourt

Weather Watcher

Materials

construction paper

crayons or markers

1. Make a book to record the weather for one week.

2. Fold three sheets of paper in half. You will have a cover and five pages.

3. Observe the weather each day. Tell about it in your book.

4. Record the outside temperature.

5. Draw a picture to show what the weather is like.

6. Share your book with the class.

Teacher's Directions

Weather Watcher

Materials   Performance Task sheets, construction paper, crayons or markers, thermometer, stapler or hole punch and yarn

Time   10–15 minutes each day

Suggested Grouping   individuals or small groups

Science Processes   observe, communicate, use numbers, use time/space relationships

Preparation Hints   Show children how to fold three sheets of construction paper in half to make a 6-page book. Staple their pages on the fold, or punch holes so they can tie them with yarn. Have them write *Weather Watcher* on the cover and label each page with the name of a school day. Place a thermometer outside the window for them to read daily.

Introduce the Task   Review with the class some different types of weather and what temperature means. Explain to children that they will be keeping a weather-watcher log. Read the directions to the children. Guide children through the first page by discussing the weather outside. Encourage them to observe the clouds, the movement of trees by the wind, the way people are dressed, etc. Repeat daily until the book is completed.

Promote Discussion   Ask children to share their books. Have them summarize the kinds of weather they observed in the past week.

Scoring Rubric

Performance Indicators

_____ Records daily outside temperature.

_____ Describes weather daily with appropriate words such as *windy*, *cloudy*, or *rainy*.

_____ Draws appropriate pictures to show what the weather is like outside.

_____ Shares observations with class by summarizing observed weather.

Observations and Rubric Score

3	2	1	0

Harcourt

The Seasons

Part I   Vocabulary

1. Write the word that completes the sentence.

A year has four _____ .

Draw a line from the words to the season they name.

2. season to plant seeds   •   • **winter**

3. season that follows spring   •   • **spring**

4. season with the fewest hours of daylight   •   • **fall**

        • **summer**

5. season that follows summer   •

Harcourt

Part II Science Concepts and Understanding

Circle the letter of the word that completes the sentence.

6. Many hours of daylight help plants grow best in the

    A winter   **B** summer   **C** fall

7. Young  are born in the

    F spring   **G** fall   **H** winter

8. In many places, leaves change color in the

    A summer   **B** spring   **C** fall

9. In which season can children play in the snow?

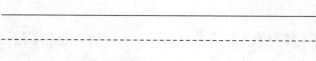

Harcourt

Name _____

For Questions 10–12, draw a line from what a farmer does to the right season for it.

What a Farmer Does

10. picks ripe fruit and vegetables •

11. plants seeds •

12. takes care of crops as they grow •

The Season

• summer

• spring

• fall

13. In which season do we see plants beginning to come out of the ground?

_____
- -
_____

Harcourt

Name _____

Part III   Process Skills Application

Process Skills: order, predict, investigate

The graph below shows the hours of light in a day.

14. Put an **X** on the name of the season that has the most hours of daylight.

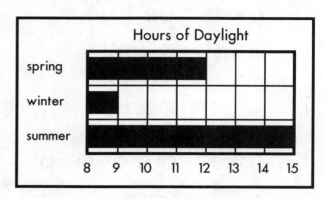

15. In which season will this squirrel look for what it is burying?

_____

- -

_____

16. Put an **X** by the best way to investigate what will grow from a seed.

___ Plant it. Put it near a window. Water it.

___ Cut it in half. Observe.

___ Try to find the seed in a book about plants.

Harcourt

Light and Temperature

Materials

stopwatch

desk lamp

thermometer

paper

Work with a partner.

1. Make a chart like this.

Light and Temperature		
Try	Time	Temperature
1		
2		

2. Place a thermometer under a lamp.

3. One person turns on the lamp. The other starts the stopwatch.

4. Try short and longer times. Record the time and temperature each time.

5. Tell what you observed.

Harcourt

PERFORMANCE TASK

Light and Temperature

| **Materials** | Performance Task sheets, stopwatch, desk lamp, thermometer, paper |

Time   20–30 minutes

Suggested Grouping   pairs

Science Processes   order, communicate

Preparation Hints   Assemble the materials. Determine the intervals of time for each try. You may wish to use 10 seconds, 30 seconds, 1 minute, and 2 minutes.

Introduce the Task   Put the headings *Summer* and *Winter* on the board. Ask volunteers to write differences they notice in the seasons (for example, in the clothing they wear, in what they can play outdoors). Be sure children think about how long the days seem during each season. Distribute materials. Read the directions aloud, and then have volunteers explain what each direction tells them to do. Repeat the activity several times, and have children record their results.

Promote Discussion   Have children share the results of their investigations. Ask them during which time period the temperature was the hottest (the longest period). Lead them to understand that the longer the period of light, the higher the temperature. Help children relate this to summer, when the days are longest and the temperatures are hottest.

Scoring Rubric
Performance Indicators

_____ Makes accurate chart for data.

_____ Turns light on and off correctly for each listed period of time.

_____ Records data on sheet accurately.

_____ Reports results to the class clearly.

Observations and Rubric Score

| 3 | 2 | 1 | 0 |

Harcourt

Investigate Matter

Part I   Vocabulary

Write the letter of the word that best completes the sentence.

A change	**C** gas	**E** liquid	**G** sink
B floats	**D** matter	**F** mechanic	**H** solid

The air that fills the tube is a **1.** ___.

The tube keeps its shape, so it is a **2.** ___.

The tube **3.** ___ on the top of a **4.** ___.

The goggles **5.** ___ to the bottom.

A **6.** ___ can fix the little boat.

Everything in the picture is **7.** ___

You can **8.** ___ an object by bending it.

Harcourt

Name _____

Circle the letter of the best answer.

9. How are these solids sorted?

   A by shape
   B by sound
   C by color

10. What is a way to measure liquids?

   F by color
   G by shape
   H by amount

11. Which object will float?

   A an anchor
   B a cork
   C a ball of clay

12. What is inside a beach ball that helps it float?

_____

- -

_____

13. Which liquids do **NOT** mix?

   F soda and water
   G oil and water
   H milk and water

Harcourt

Draw a line to what will happen.

14. If you fill
a jar with
water,   •

• it will fill up
  the space in
  in the jar.

15. If you fill
a jar with
marbles,   •

• it will take
  the shape
  of the jar.

16. If you fill
a jar with
gas,   •

• they will keep
  their shape.

17. Write two ways to classify these objects.

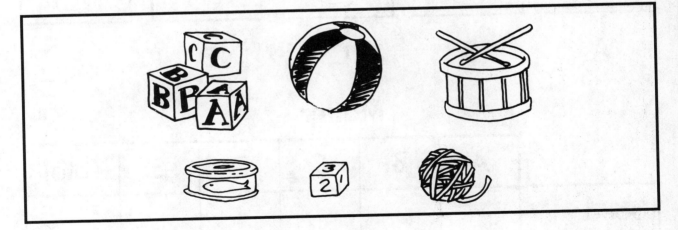

by _____

by _____

Harcourt

Part III   Process Skills Application

Process skills: collect and record data, draw conclusions

18. Put an **X** below the words that tell what does **NOT** mix.

warm water
and cold water

warm water
and ice cubes

oil and
water

___   ___   ___

19. Look at the bottles. Make a tally mark for each bottle.

A   **B**   **C**   **D**   **E**

Matter

	A	B	C	D	E	Total
Solid						
Liquid						
Gas						

Harcourt

Name _____ Date _____

Mix and See

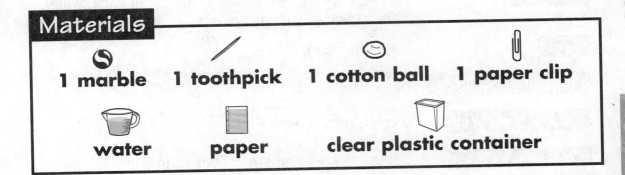

Materials

1 marble   1 toothpick   1 cotton ball   1 paper clip

water   paper   clear plastic container

1. You will put four things into water.

2. Tell what you think will happen to each.

3. Put each thing in the water. Then write **yes** or **no** to show what happened.

The Water Test

	Keeps Shape	Loses Shape	Sinks	Floats
Cotton Ball				
Marble				
Toothpick				

Harcourt

PERFORMANCE TASK

Mix and See

Materials — marbles, toothpicks, cotton balls, paper clips, water, paper, clear plastic containers

Time — 20–30 minutes

Suggested Grouping — pairs

Science Processes — predict, record data

Preparation Hints — Set up one area where children can come to get water. Assemble other materials.

Introduce the Task — Elicit the different things that can happen when objects are put into water (for example, life preservers float; anchors sink; paper things may lose their shape). Tell children that they will make some predictions about what will happen to some things when they put them into water. Distribute Performance Task sheets and materials. Ask children to read the directions silently. Then have volunteers explain the directions so that children can confirm or correct their understanding.

Promote Discussion — When children finish, ask them to share their task results with a partner. Have children tell whether or not their predictions were correct.

Scoring Rubric

Performance Indicators

_____ Writes a prediction about what will happen to the four items.

_____ Follows through on directions for immersing the four items.

_____ Records results accurately.

_____ Articulates clearly both predictions and results of immersing items.

Observations and Rubric Score

3	2	1	0

Harcourt

Name _____

Date _____

Heat and Light

Part 1   Vocabulary

Draw a line to match each word with its picture.

1. melt •

2. prism •

3. reflect •

4. refract •

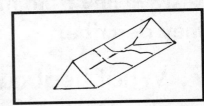

Write the word that completes the sentence.

5. The sun gives us light and

_____

- - - - - - - - - - - - - - - - - - - -

_____ .

Harcourt

Part II   Science Concepts and Understanding

6. Write an **X** under the things that give off heat.

_____   _____

_____   _____

Draw a line from the words to the pictures they describe.

7. What heat can do to gases   •

                                      •

8. What heat can do to liquids   •

                                      •

Harcourt

9. Draw a picture of
a tree reflected in
a lake.

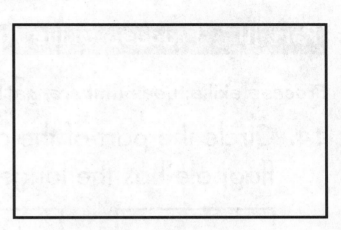

Write the letter of the correct answer.

___**10.** Light is made of many

    A gases   **B** colors   **C** prisms

___**11.** When you melt a solid, it turns
into a

    F gas   **G** light   **H** liquid

___**12.** Light may bend, or ___, where
water and air meet.

    A refract   **B** reflect   **C** melt

13. What kind of matter does boiling
water turn into?

_____

- -

_____

Harcourt

Part III   Process Skills Application

Process skills: use numbers, gather data

14. Circle the part of the day when the flagpole has the longest shadow.

morning   **afternoon**   **noon**

15. Look at the pictures and complete the chart. Write an *X* in the chart to show which cup is in the sun and which cup is in the shade.

A   B

Cup	Water Temperature	Sun	Shade
A			
B			

Harcourt

How Shadows Change

Materials

flashlight   folder   cardboard   ruler   scissors

Work with a partner. Take turns holding the flashlight and making shadows.

1. Cut out a cardboard shape.

2. Shine the flashlight on the folder.

3. Use the cardboard shape to make shadows.

4. Move the shape closer to the light. Move it farther away.

5. Measure how tall each shadow is and record the results.

6. Draw a picture to show how the shadow changes.

How Shadows Change

PERFORMANCE TASK

Materials   flashlights, folders, cardboard, rulers, scissors

Time   30 minutes

Suggested Grouping   groups of three

Science Processes   gather data, record

Preparation Hints   You may want to take the children outdoors on a sunny day with their cardboard shapes and file folders to have them use the sun as a source of light for making shadows.

Introduce the Task   Ask children about times when they see their shadows. Make sure they understand that when light is blocked, a shadow is made. Tell children they are going to make their own shadows and to experiment with what happens when the blocking shape moves closer to or farther away from the light. Ask them to predict what will happen, and write their ideas on a sheet of paper. They will need to keep the folders perpendicular to the light and the objects parallel to the folders.

Promote Discussion   Help children summarize their findings by asking them to recall how they made a shadow. Ask them to share their results and pictures from the experiments. How did they change the size of a shadow? Refer back to the predictions and ask children to compare them with their findings.

Scoring Rubric

Performance Indicators

_____ Uses a cardboard shape to make shadows of different sizes.

_____ Measures the height of each shadow and records the results.

_____ Draws a picture to illustrate change in shadow size.

_____ Explains how the size of the shadow changes.

Observations and Rubric Score

3	2	1	0

Harcourt

Pushes and Pulls

Part I   Vocabulary

Draw a line to match each word with its picture.

1. push •

2. pull •

3. zigzag •

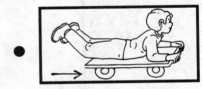

4. wheel •

Circle the word that completes the sentence.

5. A push or a pull is a

       surface   force   block

6. Moving from one place to another is called

       motion   ramp   smooth

Harcourt

7. The top or outside of something is called its

friction   **push**   **surface**

8. A force that makes it harder to move things is

pull   **zigzag**   **friction**

Part II   Science Concepts and Understanding

9. Circle the things that are being pushed.

10. Put an **X** under the animal that is moving faster.

_____   _____

Harcourt

Name _____

Circle the letter of the correct answer.

11. A path that changes directions is a

    A miss   **B** zigzag   **C** hit

12. A ball rolls farther on a

    F rough surface
    G smooth surface
    H bumpy surface

13. Put an **E** below the box that is easier to pull.

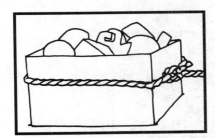 

    ___

14. Circle the surface that has more friction.

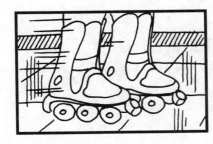 

Part III Process Skills Application

Process skills: measure, draw a conclusion

15. Look at the pictures.
Then complete the chart.

Meters Moved in One Minute

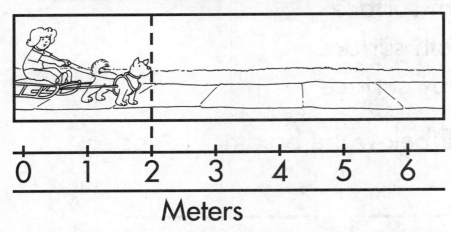

Meters

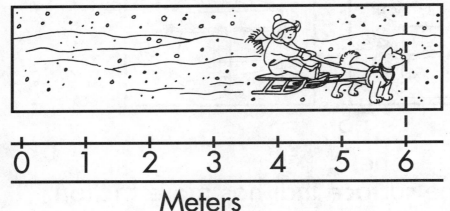

Meters

Meters Moved in One Minute

On the sidewalk	
On the snow	

Harcourt

Game of Pushes

Materials

box lid   crayons or markers   bottle cap   clay   craft stick

1. Make your box lid look like a gameboard as you see in the drawing.

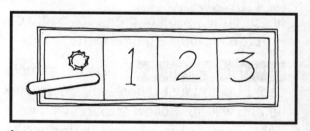

2. Use the craft stick to push the bottle cap and see where it stops. What score did you make?

3. See how many points you can score with three pushes.

4. Add a piece of clay to the bottom of the bottle cap. Try to push it again.

5. Describe the force needed to move the bottle cap with and without clay.

Harcourt

PERFORMANCE TASK

Game of Pushes

Materials — shoe box lids, crayons or markers, bottle caps, clay, craft sticks

Time — 20–30 minutes

Suggested Grouping — individuals and small groups

Science Processes — use a model

Preparation Hints — You can substitute drawing paper for box lids, checkers or small wads of paper for bottle caps, and rulers or pencils for craft sticks. Prepare a sample gameboard.

Introduce the Task — On the sample gameboard, pretend to push a bottle cap, but stop just before you do so. Ask children to predict which way the bottle cap will go. Follow through with your push so children can see if they were right. Then ask volunteers to pretend to push and classmates to predict where the bottle cap will go. Distribute the Performance Task sheets, and ask children to read the directions silently. Distribute the remaining materials. Ask volunteers to describe what they will do to complete the task.

Promote Discussion — Ask children to report their scores and their experience moving the bottle cap with and without clay stuck to it. What do children think accounted for the difference? (The clay produced friction that made the bottle cap hard to move.)

Scoring Rubric

Performance Indicators

_____ Makes a gameboard with the numbers 1, 2, and 3.
_____ Pushes bottle cap using craft stick.
_____ Records the number of points scored.
_____ Compares the amount of force needed to move the bottle cap with and without clay stuck to it.

Observations and Rubric Score

3	2	1	0

Harcourt

Magnets

Part I   Vocabulary

Draw a line from the word to the picture it goes with.

1. poles •

2. repel •

3. attract •

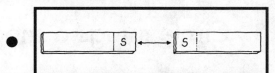

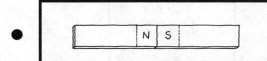

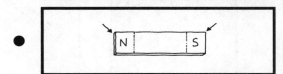

Circle the best answer.

4. A piece of iron that can pull things is a ___.

   rock   **stone**   **magnet**

5. A magnet's ___ is how strongly it pulls.

   pole   **strength**   **plan**

6. A ___ can pass through paper.

   magnetic force   **natural force**   **small force**

Harcourt

7. A magnet can give magnetic force to, or ___, things it attracts.

magnetize   **repel**   **push**

Part II   Science Concepts and Understanding

8. Circle things a magnet attracts.

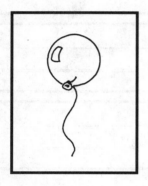   

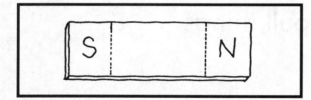 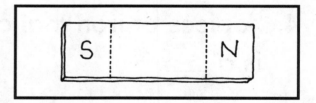

9. Which pole will attract the *S* pole of another magnet? Put an *X* on it.

10. Put an *X* on the pole that will repel the *S* pole of another magnet.

Harcourt

11. Write the word that completes *both* sentences.

All magnets have ___ in them. _____

Magnets attract objects
that are made of ___. _____

Write the letter of the best answer.

___ **12.** Where is a magnet's pull the strongest?
A at the poles
B in the middle
C near the poles

___ **13.** What can you make a magnet from?
F a crayon
G a book
H a nail

___ **14.** What kind of magnet is found in the ground?
A a gem stone
B a lodestone
C a diamond

Harcourt

Part III   Process Skills Application

Process skills: infer, investigate

15. Put an **X** by the sentence that tells what you can infer from this picture.

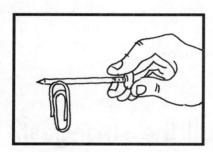

____ The nail repels the paper clip.

____ The nail has been magnetized.

16. Write 1, 2, 3 to show the order you would use to investigate how to make a magnet out of a nail.

____ See if the nail will pick up paper clips.

____ Pull the nail away from the paper clips.

____ Stroke a nail the same way with a magnet ten times.

Harcourt

Comparing Magnet Strength

Materials

two magnets   paper clips   masking tape   marker

1. Put a small piece of tape near the middle of each magnet. Write **A** on one piece of tape and **B** on the other.

2. How can you find out which magnet is stronger? Plan an investigation using the two magnets and some paper clips. Then follow your plan.

3. Draw a picture of your investigation. Put a star beside the stronger magnet in your picture.

4. Share with classmates what you found out.

Harcourt

PERFORMANCE TASK

PERFORMANCE TASK

Comparing Magnet Strength

Materials   Performance Task sheets, a variety of magnets—two different ones for each pair of children, paper clips, masking tape, markers

Time   20–30 minutes

Suggested Grouping   pairs or small groups

Science Processes   investigate, gather data, record

Preparation Hints   Each pair of children will need 10 to 20 paper clips, depending on the size and strength of the magnets.

Introduce the Task   Ask three children to select one magnet each from the assortment you have gathered. Then ask these children to demonstrate that what they selected *is* a magnet. Have them show how it picks up or attaches itself to metal objects. Brainstorm with children how they might investigate which of the three magnets is the strongest. Have children compare how well each attracts the same metal object. Distribute the Performance Task sheets. Ask one volunteer to read the directions aloud. Ask other children to explain what they will be doing.

Promote Discussion   When children finish, have the partners join others in a small group to compare their work. Have one partner in each pair describe the investigation they did and its outcome. Ask the groups to decide which of the magnets used by its members was stronger and how they know.

Scoring Rubric

Performance Indicators

_____ Plans an investigation to determine which magnet is stronger.
_____ Follows the investigation plan.
_____ Draws a picture of the investigation.
_____ Uses the picture to explain the investigation and its outcome to others.

Observations and Rubric Score

3	2	1	0

Harcourt

Name _____
Date _____

Chapter Assessment ✓

Living and Nonliving Things

Part I   Vocabulary 4 points each

Circle the word that answers the question.

1. What do we call hearing, sight, touch, smell, and taste?

ears   hands   (senses)

Circle the word that names the pictures.

2.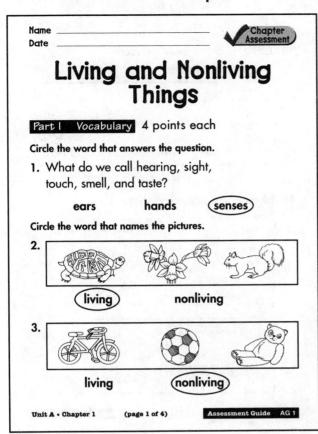

(living)   nonliving

3.

living   (nonliving)

Unit A • Chapter 1   (page 1 of 4)   **Assessment Guide   AG 1**

Name _____

8 9. Circle each word that tells what these living things need.

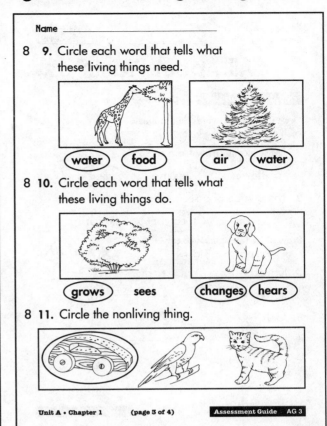

(water) (food)   (air) (water)

8 10. Circle each word that tells what these living things do.

(grows)   sees   (changes)(hears)

8 11. Circle the nonliving thing.

Unit A • Chapter 1   (page 3 of 4)   **Assessment Guide   AG 3**

Name _____

Part II   Science Concepts and Understanding

Draw a line from each sense to the child using it. 6 points each

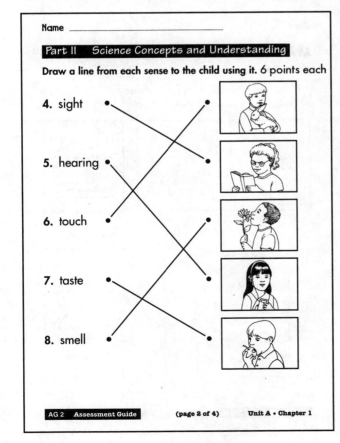

4. sight

5. hearing

6. touch

7. taste

8. smell

AG 2   Assessment Guide   (page 2 of 4)   Unit A • Chapter 1

Name _____

Part III Process Skills Application 17 points each

Process skills: observe, compare

12. Write **g** under the thing that grows.

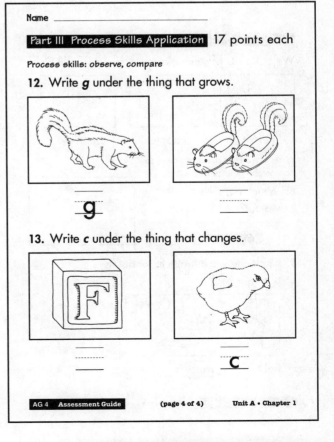

g

13. Write **c** under the thing that changes.

c

AG 4   Assessment Guide   (page 4 of 4)   Unit A • Chapter 1

Answer Key

Harcourt

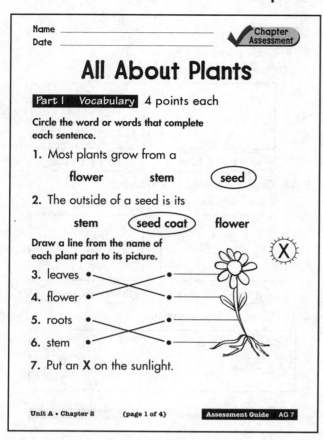

Name _____

Date _____

✓ Chapter Assessment

All About Plants

Part I   Vocabulary 4 points each

Circle the word or words that complete each sentence.

1. Most plants grow from a

   flower   stem   (seed)

2. The outside of a seed is its

   stem   (seed coat)   flower

Draw a line from the name of each plant part to its picture.

3. leaves •

4. flower •

5. roots •

6. stem •

7. Put an **X** on the sunlight.

Unit A • Chapter 2   (page 1 of 4)   Assessment Guide   AG 7

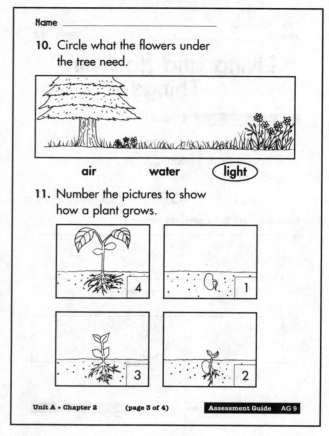

Name _____

10. Circle what the flowers under the tree need.

   air   water   (light)

11. Number the pictures to show how a plant grows.

   4   1

   3   2

Unit A • Chapter 2   (page 3 of 4)   Assessment Guide   AG 9

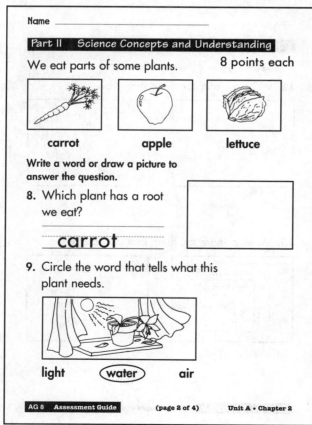

Name _____

Part II   Science Concepts and Understanding

We eat parts of some plants.   8 points each

   carrot   apple   lettuce

Write a word or draw a picture to answer the question.

8. Which plant has a root we eat?

   carrot

9. Circle the word that tells what this plant needs.

   light   (water)   air

AG 8   Assessment Guide   (page 2 of 4)   Unit A • Chapter 2

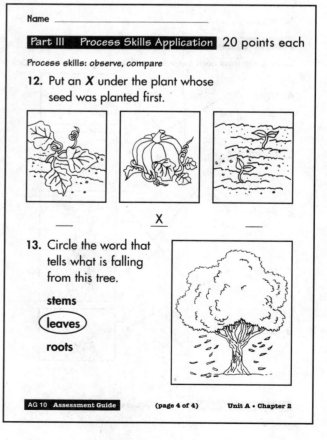

Name _____

Part III   Process Skills Application 20 points each

Process skills: observe, compare

12. Put an **X** under the plant whose seed was planted first.

   ___   X   ___

13. Circle the word that tells what is falling from this tree.

   stems

   (leaves)

   roots

AG 10   Assessment Guide   (page 4 of 4)   Unit A • Chapter 2

Harcourt

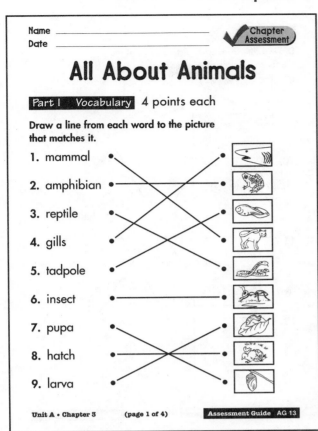

Name _____

Date _____

Chapter Assessment ✓

All About Animals

Part I Vocabulary 4 points each

Draw a line from each word to the picture that matches it.

1. mammal
2. amphibian
3. reptile
4. gills
5. tadpole
6. insect
7. pupa
8. hatch
9. larva

Unit A • Chapter 3   (page 1 of 4)   Assessment Guide AG 13

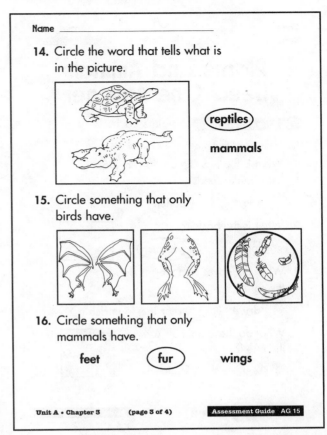

Name _____

14. Circle the word that tells what is in the picture.

(reptiles)

mammals

15. Circle something that only birds have.

16. Circle something that only mammals have.

feet   (fur)   wings

Unit A • Chapter 3   (page 3 of 4)   Assessment Guide AG 15

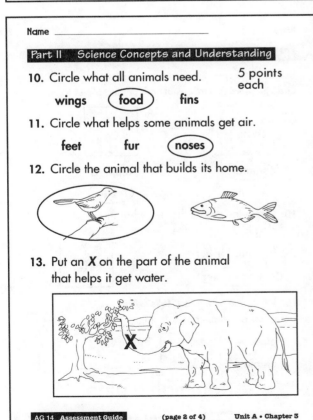

Name _____

Part II Science Concepts and Understanding

10. Circle what all animals need.   5 points each

wings   (food)   fins

11. Circle what helps some animals get air.

feet   fur   (noses)

12. Circle the animal that builds its home.

13. Put an **X** on the part of the animal that helps it get water.

AG 14 Assessment Guide   (page 2 of 4)   Unit A • Chapter 3

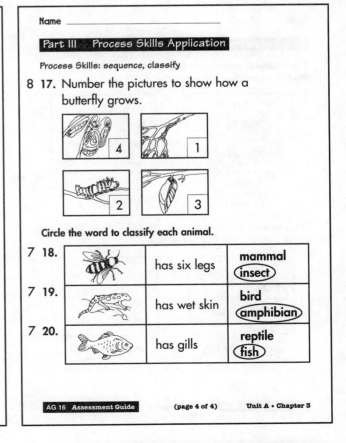

Name _____

Part III Process Skills Application

Process Skills: sequence, classify

8 17. Number the pictures to show how a butterfly grows.

4   1

2   3

Circle the word to classify each animal.

7 18.	has six legs	mammal / (insect)
7 19.	has wet skin	bird / (amphibian)
7 20.	has gills	reptile / (fish)

AG 16 Assessment Guide   (page 4 of 4)   Unit A • Chapter 3

Answer Key

Harcourt

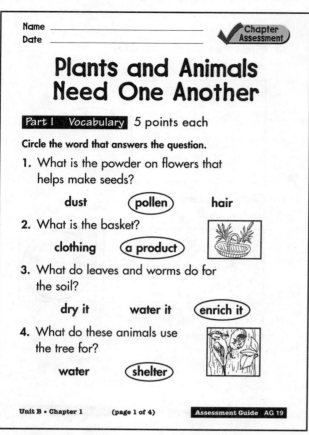

Name _____
Date _____

Chapter Assessment ✓

Plants and Animals Need One Another

Part I   Vocabulary 5 points each

Circle the word that answers the question.

1. What is the powder on flowers that helps make seeds?

   dust   (pollen)   hair

2. What is the basket?

   clothing   (a product)

3. What do leaves and worms do for the soil?

   dry it   water it   (enrich it)

4. What do these animals use the tree for?

   water   (shelter)

Unit B • Chapter 1   (page 1 of 4)   Assessment Guide AG 19

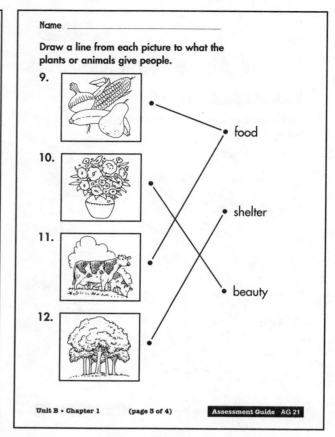

Name _____

Draw a line from each picture to what the plants or animals give people.

9. ——— food

10.

11. ——— shelter

12. ——— beauty

Unit B • Chapter 1   (page 3 of 4)   Assessment Guide AG 21

Name _____

Part II   Science Concepts and Understanding

These animals are meeting their needs with grass. **7 points** Circle the word that tells what they need.   each

5.   6.

   water   air
   (shelter)   (food)

These animals are helping plants. Circle the words that tell what they are doing.

7.   8.

   (moving pollen)   enriching soil
   finding water   (spreading seeds)

AG 20 Assessment Guide   (page 2 of 4)   Unit B • Chapter 1

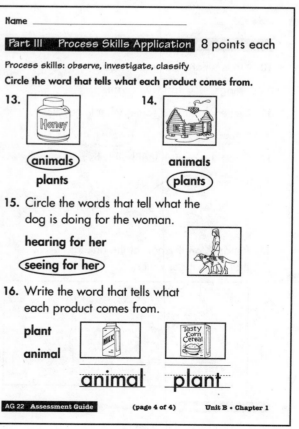

Name _____

Part III   Process Skills Application 8 points each

Process skills: observe, investigate, classify

Circle the word that tells what each product comes from.

13.   14.

   (animals)   animals
   plants   (plants)

15. Circle the words that tell what the dog is doing for the woman.

   hearing for her
   (seeing for her)

16. Write the word that tells what each product comes from.

   plant
   animal

   __animal__   __plant__

AG 22 Assessment Guide   (page 4 of 4)   Unit B • Chapter 1

Harcourt

Unit B • Chapter 2 • A Place to Live

A Place to Live

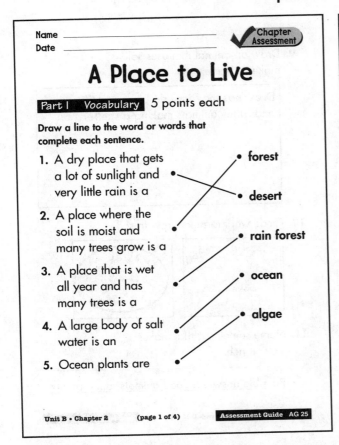

Part I **Vocabulary** 5 points each

Draw a line to the word or words that complete each sentence.

1. A dry place that gets a lot of sunlight and very little rain is a

2. A place where the soil is moist and many trees grow is a

3. A place that is wet all year and has many trees is a

4. A large body of salt water is an

5. Ocean plants are

• **forest**

• **desert**

• **rain forest**

• **ocean**

• **algae**

Name _____

Circle the words or picture to answer each question.

9. Where do some desert animals get water?

   from oceans   (from plants)

10. Which animal lives in the middle level of the rain forest?

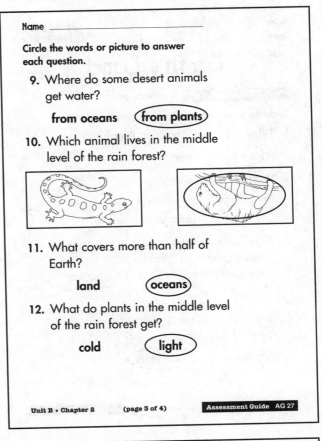

11. What covers more than half of Earth?

    land   (oceans)

12. What do plants in the middle level of the rain forest get?

    cold   (light)

Name _____

Part II **Science Concepts and Understanding**

Circle the answer to each question.   6 points each

6. What helps these plants grow in the forest?

   (moist soil)

   dry soil

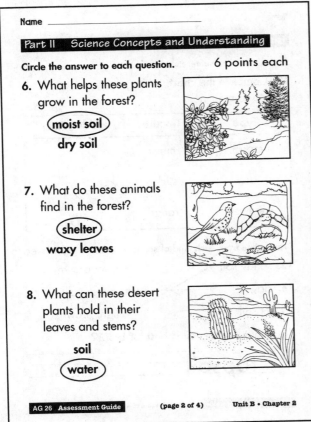

7. What do these animals find in the forest?

   (shelter)

   waxy leaves

8. What can these desert plants hold in their leaves and stems?

   soil

   (water)

Name _____

Part III **Process Skills Application**

Process Skills: classify, compare

20 13. Write letters to complete this chart. The top row has been done for you.

   d = desert   o = ocean
   f = forest   r = rain forest

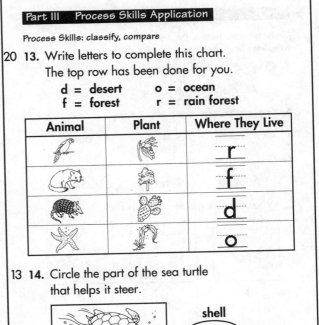

Animal	Plant	Where They Live
		r
		f
		d
		o

13 14. Circle the part of the sea turtle that helps it steer.

   shell
   (flippers)

Answer Key

Harcourt

Unit C • Chapter 1 • Earth's Land

Earth's Land

Part I   Vocabulary   4 points each

Circle the word that answers each question.

1. What is a hard, nonliving thing?

   (rock)   tree

2. What is made of very tiny pieces of rock?

   soil   (sand)

3. What is made of tiny pieces of rock and dead plants and animals?

   sand   (soil)

4. What can you find out about when you hold a rock or some soil?

   its taste   (its texture)

Unit C • Chapter 1   (page 1 of 4)   Assessment Guide   AG 31

Name _____

9. Draw an animal that uses soil to make its home.

Drawings may include birds, reptiles, and other animals making a shelter.

10. Circle what farmers grow in soil.

11. Name something that makes the soil rich.

   _____

   Possible answers: dead animals; dead plants

Unit C • Chapter 1   (page 3 of 4)   Assessment Guide   AG 33

Name _____

Part II   Science Concepts and Understanding

Circle the letter next to the word that **6 points each** completes each sentence.

5. One way to sort rocks is by their

   A smell   (B) color   C sound

6. Glass products are made from

   (F) sand   G water   H air

7. A needs soil to

   A move   B hear   (C) grow

8. What can people make from rocks?

   F   (G)   H

AG 32 Assessment Guide   (page 2 of 4)   Unit C • Chapter 1

Name _____

Part III   Process Skills Application

Process skills: compare, classify

18 12. Complete the chart. Write **y** for yes. Write **n** for no.

Type	Texture	Holds Water
topsoil	moist	y
clay	sticky	y
sandy soil	rough	n

Draw a line from each kind of soil to its color. 6 points each

13. sandy soil •   • dark brown

14. clay •   • red or yellow

15. topsoil •   • light brown

16. What kind of soil is best for crops?

   topsoil

AG 34 Assessment Guide   (page 4 of 4)   Unit C • Chapter 1

Harcourt

Name _____
Date _____

Chapter Assessment ✓

Earth's Air and Water

Part I   Vocabulary 4 points each

Draw a line from the word to the place on the map that it names.

1. lake
2. river
3. stream

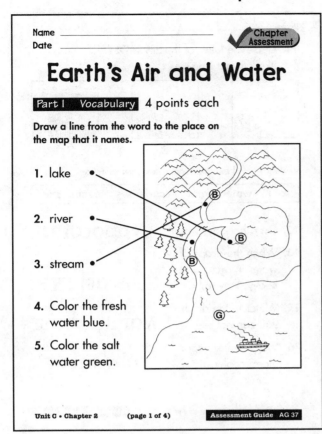

4. Color the fresh water blue.
5. Color the salt water green.

Unit C • Chapter 2   (page 1 of 4)   **Assessment Guide AG 37**

Name _____

10. Circle the picture that does **NOT** show air moving.

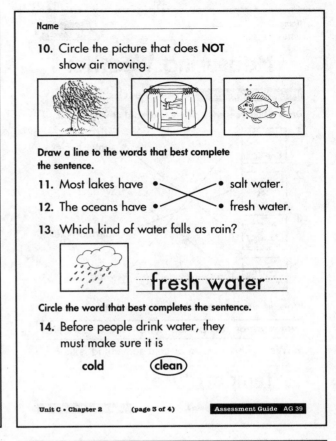

Draw a line to the words that best complete the sentence.

11. Most lakes have • ⤬ • salt water.
12. The oceans have • ⤬ • fresh water.

13. Which kind of water falls as rain?

fresh water

Circle the word that best completes the sentence.

14. Before people drink water, they must make sure it is

   cold   (clean)

Unit C • Chapter 2   (page 3 of 4)   **Assessment Guide AG 39**

Name _____

6. What do we feel when the wind blows? Circle it.

   (air)   sky   clouds

Part II   Science Concepts and Understanding

Circle the letter of the best choice. 6 points each

7. What lifts a kite into the sky?

   A clouds   B sunshine   (C) air

8. What do you know when you see bubbles in water?

   F The water is very cold.
   G You should not drink the water.
   (H) There is air in the water.

9. What must be taken out of ocean water before people can drink it?

   A clouds
   (B) salt
   C sunlight

AG 38 **Assessment Guide**   (page 2 of 4)   Unit C • Chapter 2

Name _____

Part III   Process Skills Application 7 points each

Process skills: infer, communicate

15. Circle the word that tells what is in the bubbles.

    water   (air)

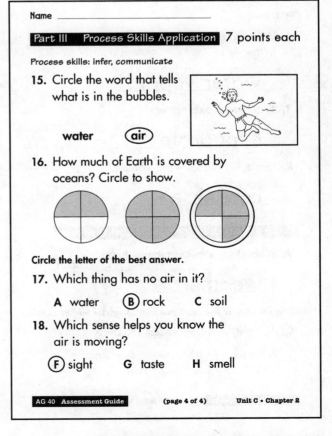

16. How much of Earth is covered by oceans? Circle to show.

Circle the letter of the best answer.

17. Which thing has no air in it?

    A water   (B) rock   C soil

18. Which sense helps you know the air is moving?

    (F) sight   G taste   H smell

AG 40 **Assessment Guide**   (page 4 of 4)   Unit C • Chapter 2

Answer Key

AG 85   Assessment Guide

Harcourt

Unit D • Chapter 1 • Measuring Weather

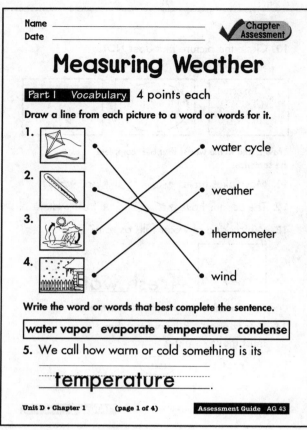

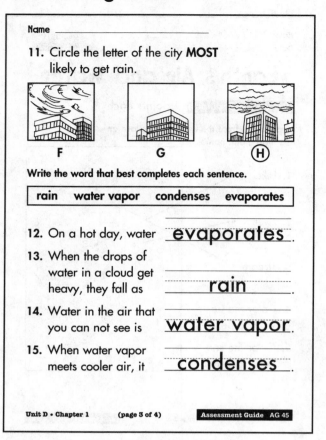

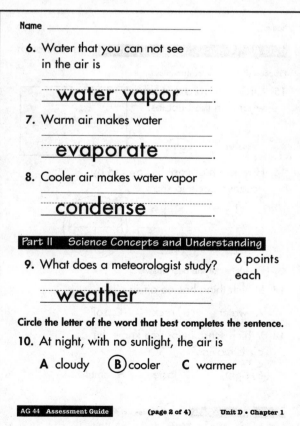

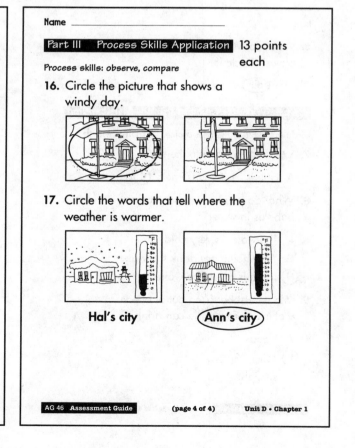

Panel 1 (page 1 of 4):

Name _____

Date _____

Chapter Assessment

Measuring Weather

Part I Vocabulary 4 points each

Draw a line from each picture to a word or words for it.

1. (kite) — wind
2. (thermometer) — thermometer
3. (water cycle) — weather
4. (rain) — water cycle

Write the word or words that best complete the sentence.

water vapor   evaporate   temperature   condense

5. We call how warm or cold something is its

temperature .

Unit D • Chapter 1   (page 1 of 4)   Assessment Guide AG 43

Panel 2 (page 3 of 4):

Name _____

11. Circle the letter of the city **MOST** likely to get rain.

F   G   (H)

Write the word that best completes each sentence.

rain   water vapor   condenses   evaporates

12. On a hot day, water   **evaporates** .

13. When the drops of water in a cloud get heavy, they fall as   **rain** .

14. Water in the air that you can not see is   **water vapor** .

15. When water vapor meets cooler air, it   **condenses** .

Unit D • Chapter 1   (page 3 of 4)   Assessment Guide AG 45

Panel 3 (page 2 of 4):

Name _____

6. Water that you can not see in the air is

water vapor .

7. Warm air makes water

evaporate .

8. Cooler air makes water vapor

condense .

Part II   Science Concepts and Understanding

9. What does a meteorologist study?   6 points each

weather

Circle the letter of the word that best completes the sentence.

10. At night, with no sunlight, the air is

A cloudy   (**B**) cooler   **C** warmer

AG 44 Assessment Guide   (page 2 of 4)   Unit D • Chapter 1

Panel 4 (page 4 of 4):

Name _____

Part III   Process Skills Application 13 points each

Process skills: observe, compare

16. Circle the picture that shows a windy day.

17. Circle the words that tell where the weather is warmer.

Hal's city   (Ann's city)

AG 46 Assessment Guide   (page 4 of 4)   Unit D • Chapter 1

AG 86   Assessment Guide

Answer Key

Harcourt

Unit D • Chapter 2 • The Seasons

Card 1 (AG 49)

Name _____
Date _____

✔ Chapter Assessment

The Seasons

Part I   Vocabulary   5 points each

1. Write the word that completes the sentence.

A year has four __**seasons**__.

Draw a line from the words to the season they name.

2. season to plant seeds •   • **winter**
3. season that follows spring •   • **spring**
4. season with the fewest hours of daylight •   • **fall**
5. season that follows summer •   • **summer**

Unit D • Chapter 2   (page 1 of 4)   Assessment Guide AG 49

Card 2 (AG 50)

Name _____

Part II   Science Concepts and Understanding

Circle the letter of the word that completes the sentence.   6 points each

6. Many hours of daylight help plants grow best in the

   A winter   (B) summer   C fall

7. Young 🐑 are born in the

   (F) spring   G fall   H winter

8. In many places, leaves change color in the

   A summer   B spring   (C) fall

9. In which season can children play in the snow?

   __winter__

AG 50 Assessment Guide   (page 2 of 4)   Unit D • Chapter 2

Card 3 (AG 51)

Name _____

For Questions 10–12, draw a line from what a farmer does to the right season for it.

What a Farmer Does   **The Season**

10. picks ripe fruit and vegetables •   • summer
11. plants seeds •   • spring
12. takes care of crops as they grow •   • fall

13. In which season do we see plants beginning to come out of the ground?

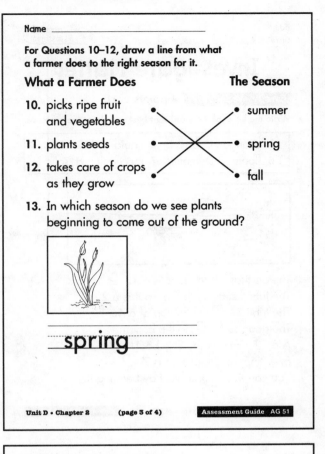

__spring__

Unit D • Chapter 2   (page 3 of 4)   Assessment Guide AG 51

Card 4 (AG 52)

Name _____

Part III   Process Skills Application   9 points each

Process Skills: order, predict, investigate

The graph below shows the hours of light in a day.

14. Put an **X** on the name of the season that has the most hours of daylight.

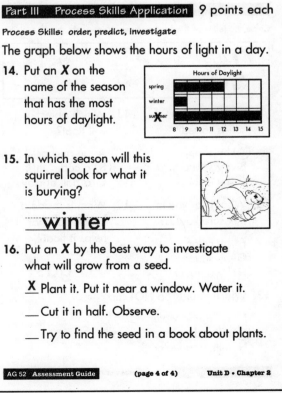

15. In which season will this squirrel look for what it is burying?

   __winter__

16. Put an **X** by the best way to investigate what will grow from a seed.

   __X__ Plant it. Put it near a window. Water it.

   ___ Cut it in half. Observe.

   ___ Try to find the seed in a book about plants.

AG 52 Assessment Guide   (page 4 of 4)   Unit D • Chapter 2

Answer Key

AG 87 Assessment Guide

Harcourt

Unit E • Chapter 1 • Investigate Matter

Name _____
Date _____

 Chapter Assessment

Investigate Matter

Part I Vocabulary 4 points each

Write the letter of the word that best completes the sentence.

A change	C gas	E liquid	G sink
B floats	D matter	F mechanic	H solid

The air that fills the tube is a **1.** _C_.
The tube keeps its shape, so it is a **2.** _H_.
The tube **3.** _B_ on the top of a **4.** _E_.
The goggles **5.** _G_ to the bottom.
A **6.** _F_ can fix the little boat.
Everything in the picture is **7.** _D_.
You can **8.** _A_ an object by bending it.

Unit E • Chapter 1   (page 1 of 4)   Assessment Guide AG 55

Name _____

Draw a line to what will happen.

14. If you fill a jar with water,

15. If you fill a jar with marbles,

16. If you fill a jar with gas,

• it will fill up the space in in the jar.

• it will take the shape of the jar.

• they will keep their shape.

17. Write two ways to classify these objects.

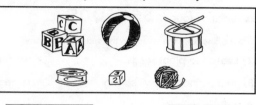

by __shape__   by __size__

Unit E • Chapter 1   (page 3 of 4)   Assessment Guide AG 57

Name _____

Part II Science Concepts and Understanding

Circle the letter of the best answer. 6 points each

9. How are these solids sorted?
(A) by shape
B by sound
C by color

11. Which object will float?
A an anchor
(B) a cork
C a ball of clay

10. What is a way to measure liquids?
F by color
G by shape
(H) by amount

12. What is inside a beach ball that helps it float?
__a gas__

13. Which liquids do **NOT** mix?
F soda and water
(G) oil and water
H milk and water

AG 56 Assessment Guide   (page 2 of 4)   Unit E • Chapter 1

Name _____

Part III Process Skills Application 7 points each

Process skills: collect and record data, draw conclusions

18. Put an **X** below the words that tell what does **NOT** mix.

warm water and cold water   warm water and ice cubes   oil and water
___   ___   _X_

19. Look at the bottles. Make a tally mark for each bottle.

A   B   C   D   E

Matter

	A	B	C	D	E	Total
Solid	I	I				2
Liquid			I		I	2
Gas	I	I	I	I	I	5

AG 58 Assessment Guide   (page 4 of 4)   Unit E • Chapter 1

Harcourt

AG 88 **Assessment Guide**   **Answer Key**

Unit E • Chapter 2 • Heat and Light

Name _____
Date _____

✓ Chapter Assessment

Heat and Light

Part I   Vocabulary 2 points each

Draw a line to match each word with its picture.

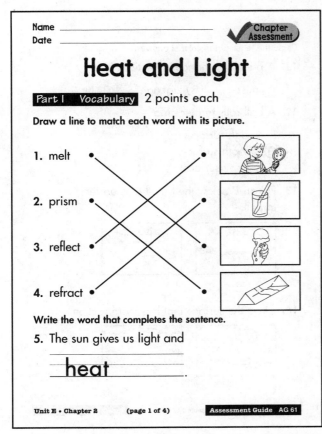

1. melt
2. prism
3. reflect
4. refract

Write the word that completes the sentence.

5. The sun gives us light and

   heat.

Unit E • Chapter 2   (page 1 of 4)   **Assessment Guide AG 61**

Name _____

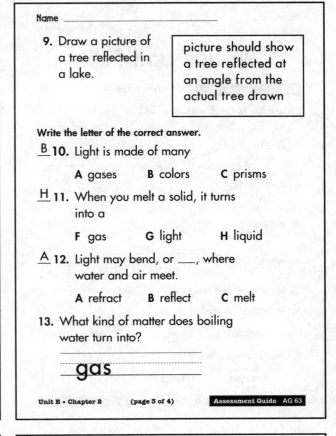

9. Draw a picture of a tree reflected in a lake.

   | picture should show a tree reflected at an angle from the actual tree drawn |

Write the letter of the correct answer.

B 10. Light is made of many

   A gases   B colors   C prisms

H 11. When you melt a solid, it turns into a

   F gas   G light   H liquid

A 12. Light may bend, or ___, where water and air meet.

   A refract   B reflect   C melt

13. What kind of matter does boiling water turn into?

   gas

Unit E • Chapter 2   (page 3 of 4)   **Assessment Guide AG 63**

Name _____

Part II   Science Concepts and Understanding

6. Write an **X** under the things that give off heat.   8 points each

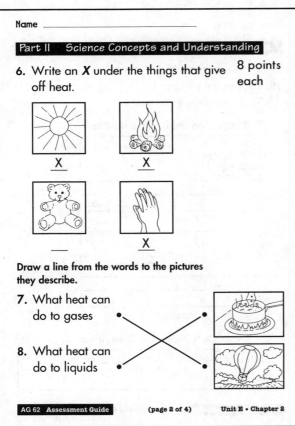

   X   X

   ___   X

Draw a line from the words to the pictures they describe.

7. What heat can do to gases

8. What heat can do to liquids

AG 62 Assessment Guide   (page 2 of 4)   **Unit E • Chapter 2**

Name _____

Part III   Process Skills Application 13 points each

Process skills: use numbers, gather data

14. Circle the part of the day when the flagpole has the longest shadow.

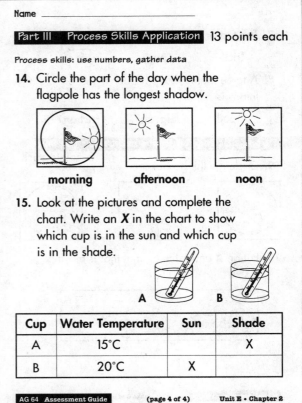

   morning   **afternoon**   **noon**

15. Look at the pictures and complete the chart. Write an **X** in the chart to show which cup is in the sun and which cup is in the shade.

   A   B

Cup	Water Temperature	Sun	Shade
A	15°C		X
B	20°C	X	

AG 64 Assessment Guide   (page 4 of 4)   **Unit E • Chapter 2**

Answer Key

Harcourt

Name _____
Date _____

Pushes and Pulls

Part I   Vocabulary 5 points each

Draw a line to match each word with its picture.

1. push
2. pull
3. zigzag
4. wheel

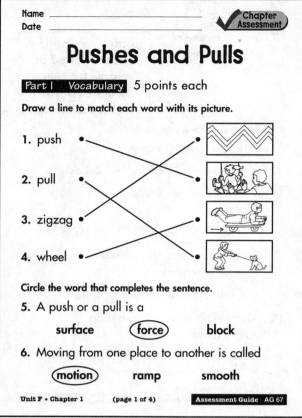

Circle the word that completes the sentence.

5. A push or a pull is a

   surface   (force)   block

6. Moving from one place to another is called

   (motion)   ramp   smooth

Unit F • Chapter 1   (page 1 of 4)   Assessment Guide AG 67

Name _____

Circle the letter of the correct answer.

11. A path that changes directions is a

    A miss   **(B)** zigzag   **C** hit

12. A ball rolls farther on a

    F rough surface
    (G) smooth surface
    H bumpy surface

13. Put an **E** below the box that is easier to pull.

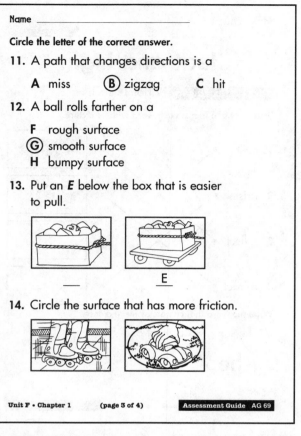

    ___   E

14. Circle the surface that has more friction.

Unit F • Chapter 1   (page 3 of 4)   Assessment Guide AG 69

Name _____

7. The top or outside of something is called its

   friction   push   (surface)

8. A force that makes it harder to move things is

   pull   zigzag   (friction)

Part II   Science Concepts and Understanding

8 points each

9. Circle the things that are being pushed.

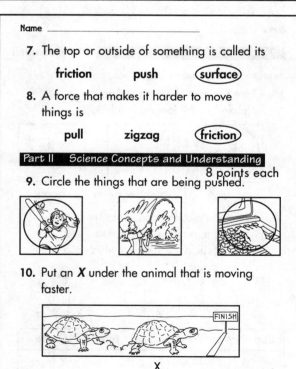

10. Put an **X** under the animal that is moving faster.

    ___   X

AG 68 Assessment Guide   (page 2 of 4)   Unit F • Chapter 1

Name _____

Part III   Process Skills Application 12 points each

Process skills: measure, draw a conclusion

15. Look at the pictures.
    Then complete the chart.

Meters Moved in One Minute

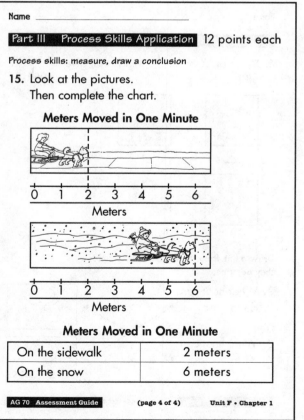

Meters Moved in One Minute

On the sidewalk	2 meters
On the snow	6 meters

AG 70 Assessment Guide   (page 4 of 4)   Unit F • Chapter 1

Harcourt

Name _____
Date _____

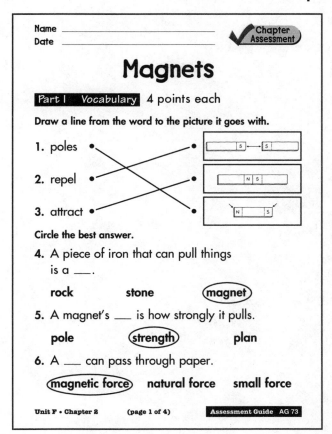

Chapter Assessment

Magnets

Part I   Vocabulary 4 points each

Draw a line from the word to the picture it goes with.

1. poles
2. repel
3. attract

Circle the best answer.

4. A piece of iron that can pull things is a ___.

   rock   stone   (magnet)

5. A magnet's ___ is how strongly it pulls.

   pole   (strength)   plan

6. A ___ can pass through paper.

   (magnetic force)   natural force   small force

Unit F • Chapter 2   (page 1 of 4)   Assessment Guide AG 73

Name _____

11. Write the word that completes *both* sentences.

   All magnets have ___ in them.

   Magnets attract objects that are made of ___.

   iron

Write the letter of the best answer.

_A_ 12. Where is a magnet's pull the strongest?
   A at the poles
   B in the middle
   C near the poles

_H_ 13. What can you make a magnet from?
   F a crayon
   G a book
   H a nail

_B_ 14. What kind of magnet is found in the ground?
   A a gem stone
   B a lodestone
   C a diamond

Unit F • Chapter 2   (page 3 of 4)   Assessment Guide AG 75

Name _____

7. A magnet can give magnetic force to, or ___, things it attracts.

   (magnetize)   repel   push

Part II   Science Concepts and Understanding

8. Circle things a magnet attracts.   6 points each

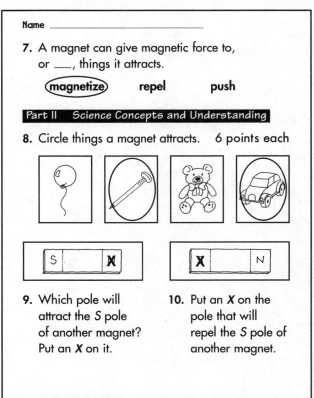

9. Which pole will attract the *S* pole of another magnet? Put an *X* on it.

10. Put an *X* on the pole that will repel the *S* pole of another magnet.

AG 74 Assessment Guide   (page 2 of 4)   Unit F • Chapter 2

Name _____

Part III   Process Skills Application 15 points each

Process skills: infer, investigate

15. Put an *X* by the sentence that tells what you can infer from this picture.

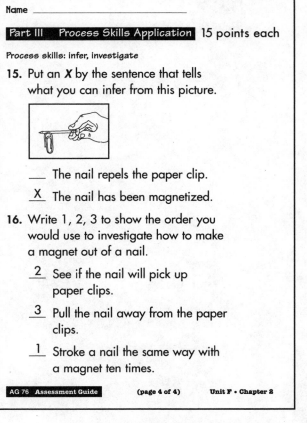

   ___ The nail repels the paper clip.

   _X_ The nail has been magnetized.

16. Write 1, 2, 3 to show the order you would use to investigate how to make a magnet out of a nail.

   _2_ See if the nail will pick up paper clips.

   _3_ Pull the nail away from the paper clips.

   _1_ Stroke a nail the same way with a magnet ten times.

AG 76 Assessment Guide   (page 4 of 4)   Unit F • Chapter 2

Answer Key

Harcourt